The road to Haworth

The road to Haworth

John Cannon

THE VIKING PRESS   NEW YORK

Copyright © 1980, 1981 by John Cannon
All rights reserved
First published in 1981 by The Viking Press
625 Madison Avenue, New York, N.Y. 10022

LIBRARY OF CONGRESS CATALOGING IN PUBLICATION DATA
Cannon, John Ashton.
The road to Haworth.
1. Brontë family.   2. Haworth, Eng.—Description.
I. Title.
PR4174.B2C36   823′.8′09 [B]   80-63662
ISBN 0-670-60079-2

Printed in the United States of America

For Cal

Contents

Illustrations

Illustrations follow page 82.

The author and publisher would like to thank Saul Barr, who took all the Irish photographs; N. K. Haworth (photographer) and the Brontë Society for 3, 8, 9, 10, 11, 12 and 13; the National Portrait Gallery for 14; and Walter Scott (photographer) and the Brontë Society for 15.

Acknowledgements

I wish to record my thanks to the many people who have helped me in the researching and writing of this book. The original idea came to me from Colin Loudan, the son of Jack Loudan, an Irish author and playwright. When Jack Loudan died, his son came across some notes and details which had been the basis of a BBC radio talk on the subject of the Irish background of the Brontë family. It is possible that Jack Loudan hoped one day to write a book on the subject. If so, my thanks must go to his spirit. Then, with the help of Robin Jasper, a retired diplomat, the basic idea was further researched and developed. In England I was greatly helped by Sir David and Lady McNeill, who made their home and library available to me; by the staff of the British Museum Library; and by the Brontë Museum at Haworth. In Ireland I received invaluable help from Mr Herbert Heslip; the staffs of Warrenpoint and Rathfriland libraries; Mr and Mrs H. Cantlie; Mrs R. Stewart and Mrs E. Rodgers; Mrs Elizabeth Brontë and many members of her immediate family; the Reverend David Neill; and the secretary of the Irish section of the Brontë Society.

All photographs were produced with the aid of Saul Barr, Rathfriland.

In addition, there are many people, professional and non-professional, who will excuse me for not mentioning them by name.

Preface

There is a story behind every book that ever came to be written, and in this respect the road to Haworth begins in 1977 on a wintry night in the Spanish province of Granada. My wife and I were tenants of an old house which stands on a rock within a stone's throw of the Mediterranean Sea. The night was stormy; the sea was pounding the stones on the beach, producing a noise very reminiscent of a night I once spent in 1947 as a young soldier at Crewe railway station. I was on my way to Northern Ireland, in the company of several equally disgruntled and unhappy young soldiers. All we knew about Northern Ireland was that it rained a lot there, and this night was especially wild and wet. We were waiting at Crewe station because we had missed a train. I tried to get some sleep on a wooden seat, but the sounds of wind and rain, blended with the hissing and clattering of trains, kept me awake. Somehow I have never forgotten that night, which should have been easily forgotten, but the mind has many mysteries.... Thirty-one years later in Spain, as my wife sat reading by the light of a butane lamp, I remembered that night. And something was about to happen that would once again link me with all those details and that would subsequently – in the most circuitous of ways – set me on the road to Haworth.

There was a knock on our door. It was late enough to be

surprising, particularly on such an intemperate night, and I opened the door to find our friends Colin and Diana Loudan. They were looking at a large slab of rock that had slid down the five-hundred-foot cliff behind the house. I assured them that a rock slide was not at all uncommon in rainy weather, but Colin's raised eyebrows reminded me that almost everyone but my wife and I considered our house a treacherous one to live in. There was also no electricity, and the water and drainage systems were shaky. But the rent was low and we had determined to make the best of it. The principal reason we were living there was that I was writing a novel with a background in rural Spain at the start of the 1936 revolution. But Colin had come with a tale that would lead to my putting aside the novel for quite a long time.

Colin and Diana had recently returned to their mountain village home, about ten miles from our own, from England, where Colin's father, the Irish writer Jack Loudan, had died. One of Jack Loudan's best-known works is the biography of Amanda McKittrick Ros, an Irish woman whose life was as strange as the books she wrote; and following the death of Jack Loudan, a BBC producer had asked his son to grant him the rights to make a television documentary about her life. Knowing that I had written for television, Colin had come to talk to me about the project.

One day, many months later, Colin mentioned to me that amongst his father's papers he had found some notes relating to the Brontë family. Jack Loudan had made the notes when he was preparing a talk for BBC radio on the subject of the Irish background of the Brontë sisters. My interest was immediately aroused. A few years before, in 1973, I had written an adaptation of Charlotte Brontë's novel *Jane Eyre* for the stage. In preparation I had studied the whole Brontë theme in depth, reading about Charlotte Brontë and her sisters and wayward brother, and also spending many hours at Haworth parsonage. But what fascinated me the most was their father, the Reverend Patrick Brontë. He was an Irishman, and I recall wondering at the time how on earth a poor Irish boy, one of ten children born to semi-literate parents, could ever have won his way to Cambridge University. But that seemed to be unimportant to the task at hand; I had a play to write, and my interest in Patrick had to be deferred. My play was later performed at Crewe Theatre as part of the Festival of British Theatre; the young soldier who had tried to get some sleep on the railway station had returned as a Playwright.

Now, four years later, Fate tugged gently at my sleeve to bring me once again into the world of the Brontë family. The conversations with Colin Loudan about his father's notes on the Brontë family reignited my curiosity, and I set out to find the answers to all the questions that had puzzled me. I wondered how these Victorian virgins came to write with such passion, and with such an implicit comprehension of the raw forces that shape human nature; or, indeed, how the three sisters ever came to write at all. But the question that ultimately seized my interest and turned it into an obsession was, Why did the Reverend Patrick Brontë do all he could to obscure his humble background? Why did he never disclose the fact that he was not born with the Brontë surname? Why did the Brontë sisters never visit their Irish relatives? Were they in fact aware that their father was born to a couple whose names were Alice and Hugh Brunty?

For two years I became a sort of literary detective. I began in Spain with the idea given to me by Colin Loudan, and one photograph of Colin's father, Jack, standing with a descendant of Patrick Brontë's mother. I also had the notes I made before beginning to adapt *Jane Eyre*. I read them again, and all the Brontë novels. Then I read again Elizabeth Gaskell's biography of Charlotte Brontë, published in 1857, which contained the first terse clues regarding the fact that Patrick did not want his own background investigated too deeply. Through friends I obtained other books, articles, and essays written at the end of the last century, and then I knew that

I would have to go to London to delve into the vast resources of the British Museum Library.

Of all the books written about the Brontë family – and there are hundreds – the one most useful to me was at the same time the most vexing. It was *The Brontës in Ireland*, written in 1893 by Dr William Wright. It contains many errors and even more digressions, yet his research took him to the area in Ireland where Patrick was born, and there Dr Wright talked to many people who knew the whole family. Although Patrick's four brothers and five sisters were dead, there were relatives and neighbours in plenty to tell him all he wanted to know about Patrick's parents, Alice McClory and Hugh Brunty.

At the heart of Dr Wright's book I found two facts upon which my own book is based. The first is that Hugh Brunty, a barely literate journeyman, enjoyed a considerable local reputation as a story-teller. Very few of his rural contemporaries could read or write, and so the oral tradition functioned, in part, to preserve what could not be written down. The art of story-telling was highly developed and by all accounts Hugh Brunty was its master. He made his living by drying corn on a simple kiln; it was by evening, around the glowing fire in his tiny cottage, that he told his tales. Like other story-tellers, his repertoire included tales, legends, and ghost-stories – tales which revealed to his friends and neighbours a glimpse of ages past in the part of Ireland where they lived.

But Hugh was a very special story-teller. Amongst all the other tales he told with such skill was what in fact amounted to his own life story. Hugh was a runaway. He had come to the area by chance, having left his home at the age of sixteen. Everything we know about him before he appeared in County Down is, in essence, one of his stories. It is only through Hugh Brunty that we know of *his* father and of the man who adopted him when Hugh's father died. All of it may have been invented by Hugh; nobody has ever been able to confirm or refute what Hugh said happened to him before he ran away. It is a tale. But we must remember that Hugh Brunty was a magnificent teller of tales, and the proof of his gift is enduring. When William Wright went to County Down, almost ninety years after Hugh had died, many of his stories – and certainly his own life story – were common knowledge. What is more, they were *believed* to be true stories.

Here I found something very startling indeed. One of Hugh's tales is about the life of his adoptive father, a man called Welsh Brunty, who was himself adopted into the Brunty family after being found abandoned as a child aboard a ship sailing from Liverpool to Ireland. The details of how this child was brought into the family, to be reared with the other Brunty children, could not fail but to recall the story of how Heathcliff was adopted in Emily Brontë's own story, *Wuthering Heights*.

The tale of Welsh Brunty was simply too well known in County Down for Dr Wright to have invented it after *Wuthering Heights* was published. I was left to draw only one conclusion. Surely Emily Brontë had heard the story of Welsh Brunty, and presumably she heard it from her father. This was the second piece of information I took from William Wright and accepted as accurate, for I could think of no other logical explanation. Now, for the first time, I began to feel what the theme of my book was to be. The Brontë sisters inherited from their father a great gift for telling tales, a talent that Patrick, in turn, had inherited from his father, and these tales appear again and again in his daughters' novels. Obviously the more I learned about the Brunty family, about the presence of an oral tradition, and about the Ireland they lived in, the nearer I came to an explanation accounting for the extraordinary narrative and imaginative gifts of the family of Patrick Brontë in Haworth. *Could* it be possible that the Brontë's rich literary kingdom had in fact been charted by their own ancestors? My mind was made up, and off we went – my wife, infant son, and I – to Ireland.

As we crossed the Irish Sea on the car ferry from Holyhead to Dublin, I was acutely aware that the journey might well be a huge disappointment. Everyone I had spoken to in Spain and in England had insisted that I would find nothing more than could be found in the books already written. But I had no desire to write a book based only on the testimony of others. I needed to 'feel' the country west of the Mourne Mountains where Hugh and Alice Brunty had lived; I wanted to see, if possible, churches, certain houses, a glen, and to see what documentary evidence remained – in church records, in local libraries – in order to put flesh on the bones of characters who were ever present in my mind. On the boat my wife and I discussed the whole project. At best we could anticipate a pleasant trip to a lovely country, but we feared, as we crossed the notorious border between Ireland's southern and northern parts, there might be some danger, too. We had accommodation booked in Warrenpoint, where, we were told, only a few days before we left England, a column of British troops from the Parachute Regiment had been attacked by the Irish Republican Army and many had been killed. We saw evidence of the attack along the road as we drove into town. English soldiers may no longer wear red coats, as in the days of Hugh Brunty, but the reason for their presence there had not changed, nor had the tragedy.

In the library at Warrenpoint I was able to examine records of the town as it was when the harbour was filled with sailing-ships. From here Patrick Brunty, aged twenty-five, had taken ship to England on the long journey that eventually brought him and his young family to Haworth parsonage. Into this harbour, according to Hugh Brunty, had sailed the ship carrying the abandoned child Welsh Brunty, who later adopted Hugh. In this town, as well, Hugh had spent a furtive honeymoon after his runaway marriage to Alice McClory, the most beautiful girl in County Down, as Hugh described her. Warrenpoint and the Brunty family were closely and fatefully connected. More than two hundred years have passed without any fundamental change in the landscape. The green hills rise up on both sides of the lough, which opens gently to the south-east and the Irish Sea. The town has a beautiful natural harbour. The prevailing winds, which are from the west, would have made the harbour an excellent one in the days of sail. Higher up the lough, towards Newry, is Narrow Water Castle, originally erected in 1212. The present structure was built in 1665. No doubt Hugh Brunty took his lovely young bride to see it as they strolled along the lough, making plans for their future.

We had been in Warrenpoint only a day or two when a chance conversation with an assistant in the library led directly to a breakthrough for me. I was given the name and telephone number of a man who, I was told, would be able to tell me a lot about the Bruntys. I called the same night. Herbert Heslip, I discovered, was a prominent member of the Irish Brontë Society. Working in liaison with Banbridge Council and the Northern Ireland Tourist Board, the society has been able to preserve many of the buildings and records relating to the Brontë family in County Down. With their help I was able to see the ruined church at Magherally where, in 1776, Hugh Brunty married Alice McClory, after eloping before her arranged marriage with a man who was, like herself, a Catholic. From there I went to the ruins of the almost unbelievably small cottage where Hugh and Alice had lived, and where Patrick Brontë was born. My wife and I spent half a day there, measuring and mentally rebuilding the cottage and sensing the texture of the life they had led there. The area is rural, even today. We imagined the cottage without modern conveniences today considered essential. 'I wonder what she used for diapers,' asked my ever-practical wife.

For many days we walked where the Brunty family had lived; in Imdel, in Ballynaskeagh; along streams running through glens as magical now as they ever were. We saw houses, churches, and schools where Patrick Brontë had started his career as a teacher, the career that led him to England and to Cambridge University. And at the end I felt I understood at last the poor Irish boy who had made his way from a humble and unlearned background to become the handsome young curate in England. I felt sympathy for his snobbery. But most important of all, I had come to know the young Patrick _Brunty_, a far different man from the tetchy octogenarian the world found living in Haworth after his last child had died. It was Charlotte Brontë who brought the family into the eyes of the world, and I realised there was a great deal of her father in who she was, and in what she wrote.

I continued to find small pieces of information that helped me to reconstruct their story. One of the most valuable of these, a record of baptisms dating from 1779, had been rescued years ago from a grocer who was using it as wrapping paper. I was able to see that book, and to photograph certain pages. My cup was already full, but through Herbert Heslip my wife and I were able to meet members of the Brontë family who continue to live within a mile or two of the place where Patrick Brontë was born. They are descendants of Patrick's brother William, but there are also branches of the family in Canada, Australia, and in the United States. One day we were entertained to tea by Emily and Anne Brontë!

Most writers have taken up the story of the Brontë family from 1820, the year when they arrived at the village of Haworth, but I decided from the beginning that my book would end at that point. My concern was the _road_ to Haworth: how the family came to live there and from whence they came. Everything I discovered and felt and saw along this road you will find in the pages to follow. However, what matters now is to explain the form in which I intend to present my story. Perhaps the simplest way of expressing my thoughts is to say that I see _The road to Haworth_ as a

series of tales forming a family saga. The tales are presented
in chronological order but are by no means heavily docu-
mented with footnotes: very few primary sources survive
and I doubt if any more will ever be found. I have attempted
here to piece the fragments together, and to use the generous
angle of Dr Wright's and Mrs Gaskell's visions, to cir-
cumvent the limitations time has imposed on the primary
sources. There is enough, however, to make me believe that
the story I am telling is as close to the truth as anyone could
get.

I decided at the outset not to tell this tale in the form of
a historical novel: I put few words into the mouths of the
characters; nor did I invent any of the plot. The first part
of my book tells the stories of Welsh and Hugh Brunty, and
ends with the birth of Hugh's first child, Patrick. All the
events here come from one source. It is the story of Hugh
Brunty's life as *he* remembered it; it is essentially legend,
and therefore asks from the reader some imaginative leap-
taking. The remainder of the book, the story of Patrick's
passage from Ireland to Haworth parsonage, is verifiable by
reference to records and in certain biographies. I have determined to tell the story of the family as an objective narrator,
and in a manner I hope would not have disappointed the
Brontë sisters' grandfather Hugh. I am quite sure, though,
that if we could hear that story in his own words, my own
attempts would be rendered pitiable indeed. As Charlotte
wrote when introducing *Jane Eyre*, 'I will tell a plain tale
with few pretentions,' and I ask you to read mine with that
preface.

The story of the road from a poverty-stricken background
in Ireland to Haworth parsonage in Yorkshire is compelling,
and in my opinion important, too. For quite clearly inside
the romance there is a clue to the genesis of the Brontë
literary tradition, and the story of their lives, and those of
their distant Irish ancestors, is also a window into a world
we have lost.

                                                                J.C.

Province of Granada, Spain   August 1980

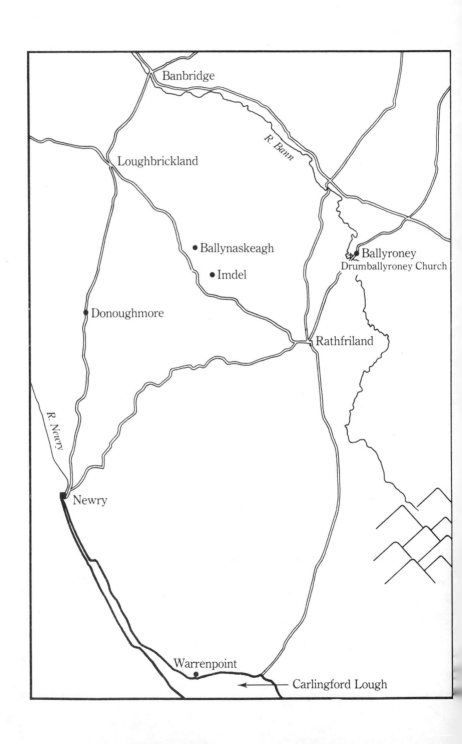

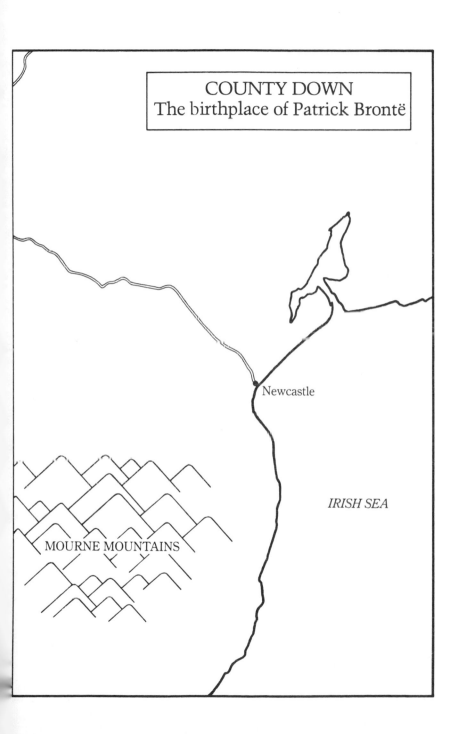

COUNTY DOWN
The birthplace of Patrick Brontë

Newcastle

IRISH SEA

MOURNE MOUNTAINS

Introduction

A neat Irish cabin, snow proof,
Well thatched, had a good earthen floor,
One chimney in midst of the roof,
One window, one latched door.

The above is one verse from a poem written by the Reverend Patrick Brontë. The poem, entitled 'The Irish Cabin', was written when he was a young man, long before his own children were born. The verse describes the house in which Patrick was born; the word 'cabin' is used instead of 'house' because his first home was extremely small. There were only two rooms. The cottage measured only eighteen feet by twelve feet. The walls were two feet thick. The building was of stone, single-storeyed; there was one door and one window. The interior was divided into two sections, the floor of each being of earth covered with straw or rushes. Today the ruins of that building are marked by a commemorative plaque stating that the father of the Brontë sisters was born there in the year 1777. The ruins stand in a rural area about twenty-five miles south of Belfast, and are one stop on a tour of what the Northern Ireland Tourist Board calls the Brontë Homeland Route.

All Patrick's children were born in Yorkshire. They lived and died in that county and wrote their novels there, and

so the County of Yorkshire has always claimed them with in-
tense pride. Their father was Irish, their mother was Cornish,
but it was the bleak, windswept moors of Yorkshire that
Charlotte, Emily, and Anne Brontë called their home.

It is one hundred and thirty four years since the first
publication of *Jane Eyre*, by Charlotte Brontë; *Wuthering
Heights*, by Emily Brontë; and *Agnes Grey*, by Anne Brontë.
Very few people knew at the time they were published that
these three novels were written by three sisters living
together in the parsonage at Haworth, each writing ener-
getically and independently of the others. Charlotte Brontë,
describing this independence, explained:

> The highest stimulus, as well as the liveliest pleasure we had
> known from childhood upwards, lay in attempts at literary com-
> position; formerly we used to show each other what we wrote, but
> of late years this habit of communication and consultation had
> been discontinued.

Charlotte was then writing an introduction to a later edition
of her sister Emily's novel, *Wuthering Heights*. She went on
to say, 'We had very early cherished the dream of one day
becoming writers.'

Their father, Patrick, had cherished the same dream. The
first work he ever published was a collection of his poems.
The first work his daughters ever published was also a small
collection of poems. Their father's poems, like their own,
were published at the author's expense. The little books were
not successful. Very few were sold, and Charlotte tells us her
reaction: 'As was to be expected, neither we nor our poems
were at all wanted; but for this we had been prepared at
the outset; though inexperienced ourselves, we had read the
experience of others.'

Who else but their father had applied the necessary caution to their hopes? Yet Charlotte, Emily, and Anne went
on writing, although they did not tell their father that they
had each decided to write a novel. When the news came that

the novels had been accepted for publication, Patrick was very surprised. He had surrendered his own hopes of ever becoming a successful author, and it seemed to him that there was little hope of his daughters' succeeding where he had failed. After all, there were very few female authors and, with this in mind, Charlotte – ever the practical one – came up with the idea of submitting their work under pen-names that belied the sex of the authors. Even their publishers were not aware of the subterfuge. As far as they knew, the novel *Jane Eyre*, which was at first by far the most successful of the three, had been written by someone called Currer Bell. *Wuthering Heights* was by Ellis Bell, and *Agnes Grey* was by Acton Bell. Charlotte Brontë explains why they decided not to use their own names:

Averse to personal publicity, we veiled our own names under those of Currer, Ellis, and Acton Bell; the ambiguous choice was dictated by a sort of conscientious scruple at assuming Christian names positively masculine, while we did not look to declare ourselves women, because – without at that time suspecting that our mode of writing and thinking was not what is called 'feminine' – we had a vague impression that authoresses are liable to be looked on with prejudice; we had noticed how critics sometimes use for their chastisement the weapon of personality, and for their reward, a flattery, which is not true praise.

Clearly it was not a device calculated to create publicity, yet it did just that. *Jane Eyre* was a success, and more; it was a novel that stirred considerable controversy. Soon, everyone wanted to know who had written the book, but the secret was kept for some time, and was only broken when one critic declared that Currer, Ellis, and Acton Bell were, in fact, one and the same. Charlotte, understandably disturbed, set off at once for London with her sister Anne, and appeared for the first time in person at her publisher's. From that moment there began an interest in the Brontë family as people. They and the lives they were living in that secluded moorland village in Yorkshire became as mesmerising as the books they had written.

Indeed, it is safe to say that there are many who know something about the Brontë story, and have not read one of the scores of books that have been written about them. The first was by Elizabeth Gaskell, who was invited by the Reverend Patrick Brontë to write 'a brief life' of his daughter Charlotte, after she died in 1855.

Elizabeth Gaskell first met Patrick Brontë when she paid a visit to the parsonage whilst Charlotte, her new friend, was still living. In a letter to one of her close friends, soon after this meeting, she recorded her impressions about him: 'I was sadly afraid of him in my inmost soul; for I caught a glare of his stern eye over his spectacles at Miss Brontë once or twice which made me know my man.' Within a very short time she was back at the parsonage; but now Charlotte was dead, and the book was written under Patrick's stern eye. With Charlotte's bereaved husband to please as well, it is a credit to Mrs Gaskell's skill that the book was ever written. As it was, she had to use a great deal of tact and caution.

The truth was that Patrick told her only as much about his family as he wanted her to know, and he evidently drew a very tight veil across his Irish background. About Charlotte and her sisters and brother he was more forthcoming. But we are nonetheless left wondering why Patrick was so determined to keep the fact of his Irish ancestry from Mrs Gaskell, and why he deliberately cut the ties between his family there and himself and his children. Was there something lurking there beyond geographical distance and a mild sense of snobbery? Does any of this further explain why the girls wrote in secrecy? Could Patrick have objected – for whatever reason – to the use of the family tales in the girls' fictions? The sources are not here keenly revealing; Mrs Gaskell's book, of course, was primarily concerned with Charlotte, and it was from the telling of *her* life story that the world first learned something about the rest of the family.

Patrick Brontë came from a very poor background in Ireland. At the age of twenty-five he went to Cambridge University in England and became a minister of the Church of England. At the age of thirty-five he married Maria Branwell, from Penzance in Cornwall, and they produced six children in as many years. The first child, Maria, was born early in 1814; the last child, Anne, was born in 1820. The following year, Patrick's wife, Maria, died at Haworth parsonage of cancer. Thus the children were raised without much knowledge of their mother; their father was the great dominating influence in their lives. In his youth Patrick was a tall, red-haired, handsome man with a reputation for charm and wit. After the sudden and painful death of his wife he became withdrawn and increasingly morose. He tried unsuccessfully to remarry, and then settled to bring up his young family with the help of his wife's elder sister. His two oldest children, Maria and Elizabeth, died tragically when they were eleven and ten years old, while his only son, Branwell, took to drink and opium, and died at the age of thirty-one. Charlotte, Emily, and Anne survived him. Within eighteen months of the publication of their books, Emily and Anne died of tuberculosis. Patrick was left alone with Charlotte. She was the only member of the family to know the pleasure of success as a writer. For a few years she developed her career as a literary figure, at the same time caring for her father, who was going blind. In 1854, at the age of thirty-eight, Charlotte married her father's curate, the Reverend Nicholls, after a considerable battle with her father, who strongly opposed the relationship. She was pregnant with her first child when she died in the following year. Patrick lived on until 1861, when he died at the age of eighty-four.

This, in the briefest detail, is the story of the Brontë family in Haworth. The parsonage there has since become a museum to their memory, administered by the Brontë Society, which was founded in 1893. The society has a world-

wide membership. In the United States there are members
in every state of the union.

The road to Haworth sets out to reveal what Mrs Gaskell
could not. It is the story of Patrick Brontë's roots in Ireland;
of his father, Hugh, who had a gift for story-telling; of
Patrick's nine brothers and sisters, who remained in Ireland;
and of their impoverished and oppressed homeland, which,
despite all its troubles, has in the rich character of its people
a wealth beyond calculation.

Our story begins somewhere about the year 1710. When
we travel this far back in Ireland, the mist of time is very
thick; there are few local records to assist us. It is a land
of legend and fable. All of what we know may be true; some
of it may be; and surely a little of it must be true, and I
have done my best to be discriminating. I feel certain there
is a strong line between the generations of Bruntys and
Brontës, and it was in this spirit that I set out on the road
to Haworth. It was there, at the parsonage, that I began.
I was hoping I might find guidance there. I was not disappointed.

Chapter 1

The first Brontë

At the beginning of the year 1820 the village of Haworth was buzzing with curiosity about the man who had just been appointed rector to the parish. In the inns of the village the latest rumours and tales were discussed every night. The men of Haworth were a dour lot; religion being as much a part of their lives as food and drink, and taken just as seriously. The previous incumbent had been appointed without due consultation with the trustees of the church and had lasted less than a month. The story of what happened to this gentleman is best told by Mrs Gaskell in her biography of Charlotte Brontë.

The first Sunday he officiated, Haworth church was filled even to the aisles; most of the people wearing the wooden clogs of the district. But while Mr Redhead was reading the second lesson, the whole congregation, as by one impulse, began to leave the church, making all the noise they could with clattering and clumping of clogs, till, at length, Mr Redhead and the clerk were the only two left to continue the service. This was bad enough, but the next Sunday the proceedings were far worse. Then, as before, the church was well filled, but the aisles were left clear; not a creature, not an obstacle was in the way. The reason for this was made evident about the same time in the reading of the service as the disturbances had begun the previous week. A man rode into the church upon an ass, with his face turned towards the tail, and as many

old hats piled on his head as he could possibly carry. He began
urging his beast round the aisles, and the screams, and cries, and
laughter of the congregation entirely drowned all sound of Mr
Redhead's voice; and, I believe, he was obliged to desist.

Hitherto they had not proceeded to anything like personal violence; but on the third Sunday they must have been greatly irritated at seeing Mr Redhead, determined to brave their will, ride
up the street, accompanied by several gentlemen from Bradford.
They put up their horses at the Black Bull – the inn close upon
the churchyard – and went into the church. On this the people
followed, with a chimney-sweeper, whom they had employed to
clean the chimneys of some out-buildings belonging to the church
that very morning, and afterwards plied with drink till he was in
a state of solemn intoxication. They placed him right before the
reading desk, where his blackened face nodded a drunken, stupid
assent to all that Mr Redhead said. At last, either prompted by
some mischief-maker, or from some tipsy impulse, he clambered
up the pulpit stairs, and attempted to embrace Mr Redhead. Then
the profane fun grew fast and furious. They pushed the soot-
covered chimney-sweeper against Mr Redhead as he attempted to
escape. They threw both him and his tormentor down on the
ground in the churchyard where the soot-bag had been emptied,
and though at last Mr Redhead escaped into the Black Bull, the
doors of which were immediately barred, the people raged without,
threatening to stone him and his friends. One of my informants
is an old man, who was the landlord of the Black Bull at the time,
and he stands to it that such was the temper of the irritated mob,
that Mr Redhead was in real danger of his life.

Mrs Gaskell goes on to record that Mr Redhead and his
friends were able to make their escape later, and that many
years afterwards he returned to preach a sermon.

The story, as told to her by an eye-witness to the events,
gives us a very clear picture of the villagers of Haworth at
that time. Elsewhere in her book, Mrs Gaskell informs us that
Charlotte told her about a local saying in Haworth: 'Keep
a stone in thy pocket seven year; turn it, and keep it seven
year longer, that it may ever be ready to thine hand when

thine enemy draws near.' Perhaps with this we are beginning
to understand what kind of people waited in Haworth to see
their new rector.

The Reverend Patrick Brontë had made sure that the trustees of Haworth accepted him. He had taken the trouble to
go there to speak with them after his appointment by the
Bishop of Bradford. Patrick would, of course, be fully aware
of what had happened to the previous temporary incumbent,
but in Patrick Brontë, the people of Haworth had a very
different man from Mr Redhead. For one thing he had come
from a background far poorer than any in Haworth village;
for another he was a very tough character indeed. Everyone
in Haworth had heard that Patrick had won his way from
a poor home in Ireland to a degree at Cambridge University
through scholarship and hard work. The Bishop of Bradford
had chosen well. If the people of Haworth were hard, then
a hard man was required to minister to them.

On an April morning in the year 1820, the family of the
Reverend Patrick Brontë had to rise very early. They had
lived for the previous five years in the parsonage at Thornton, which is now a part of Bradford, but was a separate
village in 1820. When the family first arrived in Thornton
there were two children, Maria and Elizabeth; and at Thornton four more had been born. Getting ready for the move
to Haworth must have been a very busy time for Patrick's
wife, Maria. She was thirty-seven years old; Patrick was
forty-three. Their oldest child was less than seven; their
youngest only a few weeks old. An ordinary day in the life
of Mrs Brontë must have been tiring enough, but this was
no ordinary day.

The family furniture and possessions were loaded into
seven horse-drawn carts. Then, with the family in one of the
carts, the convoy left Thornton village, taking the rough
road across the moors to Haworth. It is a distance of only
about ten miles, but it was still winter, and the weather on

the high moors is harsh. The journey would have taken two
or three hours, since it was probably raining or even snowing,
the moors bleak and windswept. John Ruskin wrote of them,
'One may lean against a Yorkshire breeze as one would
against a quickset hedge.' Mrs Brontë was tired before the
journey began; she was in poor health and already suffering
from the illness which would take her to her grave within
two years. It was to prove the last time she or any of her
family would ever have to move house.

The Brontë children were excited at the prospect of a new
home. The parsonage at Haworth was a much bigger house
than the one in which they had been living. Their father had
told them about the village, and the moors which surrounded
it, and even in the grip of winter the moors have a magic
about them, a quality of space and wilderness which is inspir-
ing. In spring and summer the air is filled with the sounds
of wild birds. There are flashing streams running down the
valleys; hares and rabbits and foxes abound; hawks and fal-
cons soar in the broad sky.

For the Reverend Patrick Brontë, this move to Haworth
was promotion, and he was looking forward to the responsi-
bilities which awaited him there. In his diary he wrote: 'My
salary is not large; it is only about £200 a year. I have a
good house, which is mine for life also, and is rent-free. No
one has anything to do with the church but myself, and I
have a large congregation.'

The house to which he was bringing his family was a solid,
four-square structure of Yorkshire sandstone, almost like a
child's picture of a house, with a door in the middle, two
windows either side, and five in a line above. It was lit by
candles and oil lamps, and water was supplied to the kitchen
by a handpump. The outlook from the front of the house
was stark; it faced the churchyard filled with graves and
headstones. But all this must be viewed in perspective. It
was the finest house that Patrick Brontë had ever lived in;
and indeed it was a grand house compared with those in the

village. Patrick must have been aware that the area was un-
healthy, since the average life expectancy was less than
thirty years. Half the children died before reaching the age
of six. There had been frequent outbreaks of typhus, cholera,
dysentery, and smallpox; tuberculosis was common. Patrick
lived to be eighty-four, but his wife and all his children died
young. Mrs Maria Brontë was already suffering from cancer
when she arrived in Haworth, but the cold and the damp
there may have accelerated her illness. The early deaths of
all her children may be attributed to the living conditions
in the area at the time.

It is not difficult to picture the scene as the seven horse-
drawn carts trundled across the moors on that April day.
About forty years later, when Mrs Gaskell arrived in
Haworth to write Charlotte's biography, it is unlikely that
the village had changed much, and so when we read Mrs Gas
kell's fine description of the approach to the parsonage we
can, in effect, see what the Brontë family saw as they arrived
in Haworth.

For a short distance the road appears to turn away from
Haworth, as it winds round the base of a shoulder of a hill; but
then it crosses a bridge over the 'beck' and the ascent through the
village begins. The flag-stones with which it is paved are placed
end-ways, in order to give a better hold to the horse's feet; and
even with this help they seem to be in constant danger of slipping
backwards. The old stone houses are high compared to the width
of the street, which makes an abrupt turn before reaching the
more level ground at the head of the village, so that the steep
aspect of the place, in one part, is almost like that of a wall. But
this surmounted, the church lies a little off the main road on the
left; a hundred yards or so, and the driver relaxes his care, and
the horse breathes more easily, as they pass into the quiet little
by-street that leads to Haworth parsonage. The churchyard is on
one side of this lane, the schoolhouse and the sexton's dwelling
(where the curates formerly lodged) on the other. The parsonage
stands at right angles to the road, facing down upon the church;

so that, in fact, parsonage, church, and belfried schoolhouse, form
three sides of an irregular oblong, of which the fourth is open to
the fields and moors that lie beyond.

At the parsonage, two house-servants were waiting to
greet the Brontë family. They were the servants from Thornton who had gone ahead a few days before to get the parsonage at Haworth ready for their master's family. They
have been described as 'two rough, warm-hearted sisters',
and we can imagine the interest they would be taking in their
charges. Mrs Brontë, a small, neat woman, with a great deal
of quiet charm; the children – Maria, not quite seven; Elizabeth, approaching six; Charlotte, almost four; Patrick Branwell, two and a half; Emily Jane, eighteen months; and
Anne, still a babe in arms – and the Reverend Patrick, tall,
lean, red-haired, dressed in clerical black. All of them were
quickly ushered into the parsonage, where fires were burning,
and no doubt hot drinks were soon provided. It was decided
that the parlour to the left of the entrance door should be
the family sitting-room and the room on the right of the entrance, Patrick's study. The stone-flagged kitchen was at the
rear of the house, from which a door led into a small garden
and the moors beyond. Upstairs were four bedrooms and a
tiny room over the entrance passage which, it was decided,
should be called the 'children's study', for Patrick was a
great believer in education beginning as soon as possible.

His own study was barred to the children. Even his
wife and the two servants entered Patrick's study very
rarely. There, he would write his sermons and his letters, and
read his papers. There also, and quite apart from his
parochial duties, Patrick Brontë intended to work at his
creative writing; for he was determined to get his name into
the annals of British literature. He had been writing poetry
since he was a young and penniless lad in Ireland and already
there were four volumes of his poetry and prose in print. But
of late, Patrick had begun to think that perhaps something

more substantial might be aimed at. At this stage of his life, Patrick saw his six children as a hindrance to his personal ambitions, finding it more and more difficult to write. He was quite sure in his own mind, however, that if anything of importance was to be achieved by the Brontë family, it would have to come from himself or his only son, Branwell.

His lifelong desire to be accepted as a poet, author, and man of letters rested on his own sure knowledge that he had been born with a great talent. Patrick's father, Hugh, was talented but he was barely literate, and so it was impossible for him to translate his thoughts into the written word. In fact the little writing done by Hugh – a few poems – was edited by his son Patrick after the old man had died. The talent which Hugh had was that of a great story-teller, who could tell a story in such a way that his audience was enthralled. We should remember that in every culture, before there is general literacy, the story teller is a great entertainer. Most of the great stories from the past were handed down from generation to generation by word of mouth, long before they were ever set down in writing. Legends, romances, fairy-tales, ghost-stories are verbal novels. The talent of story-telling goes back far into the history of man; and there are cultures, even today, where the story-teller is as much a part of society as is the witch-doctor and the medicine-man. Patrick Brontë's father was a renowned story-teller, and Patrick grew up listening to his father's tales; observing the reactions in his audiences. He inherited the gift of being able to hold an audience with words, which is, after all, the combination of the ability to 'see' a good story and the facility to tell it. In his case, because he became a preacher, the talent was utilised in telling the story of Christianity, and Christ's message to mankind. Patrick was certainly a very good preacher, as many who listened to him have recorded. Frequently, in the church at Haworth, Patrick spoke for well over an hour without using notes. One diarist wrote, 'The moment he climbed into the pulpit, a spell was cast over the whole congregation, and no-one moved.' We encounter his gift again when we read in Mrs Gaskell's biography of Charlotte Brontë that Patrick often told his children, '... weird Irish tales in such a manner that all the children were often held spellbound.'

It has often been said that Patrick was a tyrannical father who resented his children's presence. This is certainly untrue; he was always concerned for his children. True, he wanted them all to learn to live frugally, but he believed this was a good principle, and he did not exempt himself from it. He was particularly concerned about the intellectual development of his children, providing them with books, art and music lessons, but above all the desire to make a name for themselves. Natural talents have to be developed by study and application. This was the message he gave to his children – the message that his father had given to him. It is a characteristic of Celtic people to have a love and a respect for learning, and all the Brontë children showed a great desire for learning. Only Charlotte lived to see success, but her sisters never stopped trying for it. This great driving force to *do* something with life is seen, perhaps at its most heartbreaking, in a letter from Anne Brontë to a friend. It was one of the last letters she was to write before her death at the age of twenty-nine.

... I wish it would please God to spare me, not only for Papa's and Charlotte's sakes, but because I long to do some good in the world before I leave it. I have many schemes in my head for future practice – humble and limited indeed – but still I should not like them all to come to nothing, and myself to have lived to so little purpose.

At this point it is necessary to draw back a little from the picture of Patrick and Maria with their children in the parsonage at Haworth, for that is the end of the road. The beginning of the road is in Ireland. A great deal is known about the father and mother of Patrick Brontë; and although much less is known about *their* families, what is known can serve as a beginning to the road which leads to Haworth. The tracing of a family history is always interesting, and all the more so when we find a Charlotte, or an Emily, or an Anne Brontë, at the end of it. In Ireland we find that Patrick's father, Hugh, had a great reputation as a story-teller. In his book, *The Brontës in Ireland* (1894), Dr William Wright says, 'Hugh seems to have had the rare faculty of believing his own stories, even when they were purely imaginary; and he would sometimes conjure up scenes so unearthly and awful that both he and his hearers were afraid to part company for the night.'

We already know that Patrick inherited this faculty from his father. It is fascinating to follow this through to his children, and to find in a letter written by Miss Ellen Nussey, a schoolmate of Charlotte's, this description of why Charlotte was in great demand as a teller of dormitory thrillers in the school.

She brought together all the horrors her imagination could create, from surging seas, raging breakers, towering castle walls, high precipices, invisible chasms and dangers. Having wrought these materials to the highest pitch of effect, she brought out, in almost cloud-height, her somnambulist, walking on shaking turrets.

It seems that Charlotte could tell stories then as well as she later came to write them! And by all accounts Charlotte was the least imaginative of the children. One wonders what kind of stories Emily, with her wild mind, might have told when she chose to? In the book *The Brontë Story* by Margaret Lane, the author makes this assertion:

It is rare to find genius in a family which has given no hint or promise of its coming, and in Mr Brontë's poetic musings and little prose works, worthless though they are, and in his passion for literary composition, we perceive that craving for self-expression which was to inflame and exalt his children like a fever; and in the Spartan ambition which had lifted him from a poor Irish cabin and brought him through Cambridge to his present clerical dignity and scholarly retirement, that resolution and self-discipline which was a part of his daughters' greatness.

There can be no quarrel with any of that, except that now we may be able to see the genius appearing in many forms.

But there is another reason for delving back into the past. Patrick's father, Hugh, told a tale of his childhood, about his adoption by a man who was himself adopted into the family. The story may, or may not, be a true one. In the area of the mountains of Mourne where Hugh lived, truth and fiction often dance a jig with each other, and it is difficult to see which is which, but in the case of this particular tale it matters not whether it is true or wholly imaginary. The point is that the tale was known to Patrick. He had heard his father tell it many times, and, in fact, the story amounted to his own family background. All of us are interested in knowing where we come from, and it is highly probable that Patrick told his children his version of the same story. Even if he prefaced the story with a warning that it might not be true, the tale is compelling enough to have fixed itself in the imagination of his children. There, in Haworth, sitting before a blazing fire in the evening, Patrick told his children about their grandfather, and what happened to him as a child and a young man. It is the sort of story all children love to hear. And the picture of a man telling stories around a fire is central to the theme of this book. Hugh told *his* stories around a fire. He had built a corn-drying kiln in his cabin, and the story-telling was done in the light and warmth of the glow from the fire.

The point we are coming to is that there are certain connections between the stories of the Irish family background and the story of *Wuthering Heights*. Emily Brontë, being the most impressionable of Patrick's children, was intrigued by the story of her grandfather; and when she came to trying

her hand at a novel, her inspiration began there. This takes
nothing away from *Wuthering Heights*, rightly considered to
be a classic and the only novel Emily ever wrote. But the
other sisters wrote their novels against a background of experience and fact ; and it is possible that Emily did the same.
The adoption of Heathcliff into the Earnshaw family, which
might be regarded as the starting point of the story told in
Wuthering Heights, is very similar to a tale about the Brontë
family in Ireland. Emily might have used this tale with
others she heard in Yorkshire when she set out to write a
novel. The similarity of the two stories is far too great to
be ignored.

There can be no doubt that the Brontë sisters learned
much from their father, and not least the experience he
gained in his own life, passed on to his children in the form
of stories. After all, their own experience was comparatively
limited. But the more we know about Patrick, the more we
can see of him in the characters of his daughters and also
in their work.

When considering Patrick's influence on his children, it
must be remembered that their mother died when they were all
very young. Maria was a gentle woman, brave and kind, but
none of her children really knew much about her, apart from
what they were told. When their mother died, Charlotte was
five, Emily was two and a half, and Anne was only a year
old. The *image* of their mother was strong in their minds,
and it is often seen in the fictional characters which the girls
created, but they were all far too young to be influenced
by her in any other way. Maria's sister became a surrogate
mother to the children but her influence is not considered
to be profound. On the other hand, Patrick, with his charis-
matic personality and his dominance in the household, was
beyond any doubt the major influence on the lives of his
children. They had few friends in the village, since they were
almost always together in a tight family group inside the parsonage. They lived so close together that, as children, they

invented a fantasy world all of their own. As they grew older, Branwell found friends away from the family, but on the whole the girls did not. They travelled little; and when they did they were unhappy. The more one reads about their lives, the clearer becomes the picture of three shy, introverted, unworldly girls, living in the shade of their father's will and dominance. Patrick's ideas, his morality, and his passion can be found in every Brontë novel. For this reason alone, the more we know about Patrick and his background, the better we can come to a fuller understanding of their works.

Patrick was not born Patrick Brontë. Although we know he was born in Ireland, near the village of Ballynaskeagh, about eight miles north-east of Newry, the record of his birth has been lost. The parish register does, however, contain an entry for his brother William, who was born two years after Patrick. That entry reads: '1779, March 16, William, son of Hugh and Elinor Brunty, Ballyroney'. The register contains entries for five more children born to the same parents. There were, in all, ten children, but the records of four of them cannot be found. Of the six entries in the register, now kept in the church at Ballyward, five are written 'Brunty', and one 'Bruntee'. The first page dates from 1779, when the birth of William Brunty is clearly recorded. On later pages are entries for Hugh, James, Welsh, Jane, and Mary who was born in 1791. Also in the register is an entry showing the birth of a son to the Reverend Thomas Tighe, who was of such importance to Patrick Brontë in later years.

When he went to Cambridge in 1802, Patrick's name was recorded as Patrick Branty. The hand-written registers containing these entries were, of course, all written by clerks who made their own decision as to how the name was spelled, but before Patrick went to England the name was never written 'Brontë'. Branty is an Irish name; so is Brunty, but Brontë is not, and never has been. Whilst at Cambridge, Patrick took to signing his name Patrick Bronte, later adding the stress above the final letter, making it clear that the surname should be pronounced Brontë, and not Bront. This could have been achieved by writing the name as 'Bronty'. In other places we even find the name is written as 'Prunty'. Therefore we have for our choice, Brunty, Bruntee, Branty, Prunty, and Brontë, but we must remember that spelling was notoriously bad in the eighteenth century. For example, two place-names which figure in the life of Patrick Brontë are often written with different spellings: the village of Ballynaskeagh is written as 'Ballynasceagh' by Patrick himself in a letter to his brother who was living there. Sometimes the name is written as 'Ballinaskeagh'. And the nearby hamlet of Emdale is often written as 'Imdel'. This accounts for some of the inconsistencies, but there is another interesting possibility. Patrick entered the College of St John's, Cambridge, in 1802. He was admitted as a 'sizar', that is to say as a poor scholar. In St John's College magazine, *The Eagle*, volume XVIII, dated 1895, we find the following: 'A remarkable fact becomes apparent, that in the period covered by this register – not a time for which we look with enthusiasm in the cause of either learning or philanthropy – many poor men's sons found their way to St John's.'

The article in the college magazine is discussing the publication of their register of admissions, and it goes on to say that the College of St John's had fulfilled its mission of uniting class to class. Whether we can accept that is immaterial; what we can be sure of is that Patrick went to Cambridge as a poor scholar, the son of a poor man, and everyone knew that, but Patrick was a proud man throughout his life. Arriving at Cambridge, probably in his homespun clothing, and with an Irish brogue, he must have been a rare figure. When asked his name by the Registrar, Patrick gave it, and the Registrar wrote that name as Patrick Branty. But if the names Branty, Brantee, Brunty, Prunty, or Bronty are spoken in the accent of the north of Ireland, they all *sound* the same. Patrick Brunty ... or Patrick Brontë? There is no way of knowing for certain how Patrick wrote his name *before* he left Ireland, but soon after enrolling at Cambridge he began to write his name as Bronte. At that time he did not add the diaeresis; that affectation came later. Patrick merely signed himself Patrick Bronte, and this made no difference at all to the way he pronounced his name. By a coincidence, however, in the year 1801, the year before Patrick entered Cambridge, Admiral Lord Nelson – possibly the greatest hero-figure that Britain has ever known – was granted the permission of his Sovereign to assume the title of Duke of Brontë, an honour given to Lord Nelson by the grateful King of the Two Sicilies. Brontë is an estate in Sicily, near to Mount Etna. Admiral Lord Nelson, Duke of Brontë, Patrick Brontë; the name carried prestige, and, after all, Patrick was not changing his own name, merely insisting that henceforth it should be spelled in a particular way. And so he became the Reverend Patrick Brontë; and his daughters are the Brontë sisters, when they might well have been the Brunty sisters.

Today, of course, this matters little, but in Patrick's lifetime it mattered a great deal. He went to some trouble to make sure that his name was spelled this way. When he writes to his family in Ireland he spells their name as 'Brontë', although they continue to spell it as 'Brunty' or 'Branty'. Patrick convinced himself he was Patrick Brontë; and in time everyone came to accept that that was his name. As a link with his great hero, Lord Nelson, the name carries distinction, whereas Brunty does not, and yet we must remember that, as spoken in the north of Ireland, the two names sound exactly the same.

After obtaining his degree at Cambridge Patrick paid one visit to Ireland to see his family, and he continued to correspond with them irregularly throughout his long life. Yet in the correspondence of his daughters – and there is a great deal of this on record – there is no mention of them ever meeting their relatives in Ireland. There is a tale of Patrick's

brother Hugh going to England after *Jane Eyre* was
published, but if this is true Charlotte made no mention of
it in her letters. In fact there is only one fragment of evidence
to suggest that any of the family in Ireland were known to
Patrick's children. It is contained in a note from Ellen Nussey, Charlotte's schoolfriend, written to Mr J. Horsfall-
Turner, who edited a collection of Patrick Brontë's poems
and stories. 'Charlotte described an uncle from Belfast, who
visited them, as a staid and respectable yeoman, of good personal appearance, and she also spoke of an aunt Collins, of
whom she knew little, to her regret.' Two of Patrick's sisters
were twins, Rose and Sarah, and the latter married a man
called Simon Collins.

It is interesting to note that when Charlotte married her
father's curate, the Reverend Nicholls, who was an Irishman, the newly-weds went to Ireland to spend their honey
moon, but they made no attempt to visit Charlotte's relatives. At that time, eight of Patrick's nine brothers and
sisters were still alive. Of course, travel was not easy then,
and the honeymoon was spent in the south of Ireland, but
even so there is some reason to believe that Patrick did not
wish his daughter to visit the family. Charlotte died within
a year of being married, and, soon after that, Patrick invited
Mrs Gaskell to write the biography of the daughter who had
become a literary figure. Mrs Gaskell was a writer of some
repute, and she had known Charlotte for the last few years
of her life. She was made welcome at Haworth and given
every possible assistance but, when she came to ask questions about the family in Ireland, we can see that very little
information was forthcoming.

In her introduction to the biography, Mrs Gaskell writes:
'The family with whom I have now to do shot their roots
down deeper than I can penetrate.' That little comment says
a great deal. It appears to be less than completely truthful
because, had Mrs Gaskell wished to write about the family
background, there would have been little difficulty in finding

all she wanted to know. Had she visited Ireland at that time, she would have found that Patrick's father was a legend there. She would have found Patrick's brothers and sisters willing to tell her about the family roots. She would have found many friends of the family who had known Hugh Brunty and his Catholic wife, Alice, and had heard from Hugh the whole story of the family, going back to Charlotte's great-great grandfather! It is impossible to believe that Mrs Gaskell overlooked this opportunity. She was far too experienced a writer to make that mistake.

Mrs Gaskell's statement would be a truthful one if she had said that she decided not to dig up the family roots; and the only reason for that decision could be that Patrick's wishes were being respected. Perhaps Mrs Gaskell realised that by leaving the Irish family background unexposed, she would find Patrick all the more helpful when it came to talking about Charlotte, the subject of the biography. She would not be the first biographer to have employed discretion.

Chapter 2

Welsh's story

In 1894 Dr William Wright published his biography of the
Brontë family, which he entitled *The Brontës in Ireland*, a
task for which he was well qualified. One of his classical
teachers was the Reverend William McAllister, who had
known Patrick Brontë, and also had memories of how Hugh
Brunty could hold an audience enraptured, with the tales
of his youth. Dr Wright also talked with relatives of people
who had heard the tales. There were slight differences
between the tales as remembered by one person or another,
but in general, the main group of tales, which were Hugh's
own account of his background, were more or less the same.
Dr Wright also knew the Reverend David McKee, who was
then living in the Manse at Ballynaskeagh, and was a close
friend of many of the Brontë family still living there. From
Dr Wright's book, therefore, we can extract a great deal
of information which came to him from people who had
actually heard Hugh Brunty telling his tales, or from the
children of such people who had been told about the tales.
Since Dr Wright wrote his book, others have followed;
and for my part I have tried to make a shrewd guess as
to what is truth and what is fancy. The tales now follow.
Try to imagine the young Brontë children, sitting around
the fireplace in that solid house at Haworth, sheltered

from a howling wind outside, and asking their father
to tell them a story ... the story of their grandfather in
Ireland.

In about the year 1710 the grandfather of Hugh Brunty, a
cattle-dealer, made a journey to England. At this time there
was a lively cattle trade between Ireland and England, and
there was a regular sailing of a packet-boat between Warrenpoint in County Down and Liverpool in England. Old Hugh
Brunty, who had his own farm somewhere near Newry, was
a regular passenger on these voyages. His business was to
act as middle-man between the farmers in the area where
he lived and the busy cattle market in Liverpool. Apparently
he was good at his job, and also a popular figure, which says
a lot for the way he conducted his business. Hugh was
married, with three children, at the time when he made this
particular voyage to Liverpool. The journey was only one
of many he had made, but it became one he would never
forget for two reasons. The first reason was unusual enough,
because he took his wife with him, although he had never
done so before. The small sailing-ship had very little in the
way of accommodation for passengers. The cattle were
stowed on deck together with the farmers handling them.
The ships were old, had seen better days and were now serving out their time as cattle ships, making the relatively easy
passage between Ireland and England. I say relatively,
because the Irish Sea is notorious for its vagaries; nevertheless the passages were only a matter of hours if the winds
were fair. At worst it meant no more than the best part of
a day spent in discomfort, and for the farmers this was nothing unusual. But for women making the journey it was a very
different matter; and few did. Apart from anything else,
women were considered to be a bad omen when they were
aboard a ship at sea. When the ship was in harbour, then
matters were very different. But on board a sailing-ship leaving harbour and heading for the open sea, the presence of

a woman was enough to make any sailor shake his head and make ready for rough weather.

As it happened the voyage to Liverpool from Warrenpoint was calm and undistinguished in any way. Hugh Brunty did his business in the cattle market, and his wife had a rare treat shopping in the city. It was on the return voyage from Liverpool to Warrenpoint that there occurred something which was to have its effect on the Brunty family for generations. Soon after the ship left Liverpool harbour, but long enough to deter the captain from returning there, one of the crew discovered a young child hidden in the hold, dirty and wrapped in rags. There was no way of determining how it came to be aboard, but it was presumed to be the child of some woman in Liverpool who cared nothing for what happened to it. It was a male child, with dark hair and skin, and was thought to be a gypsy. There was of course no doctor on board the ship, and when it was suggested that the child may have been abandoned because it was diseased in some way, there was a general outcry to throw it overboard. It is probable that this would have happened but for the presence of Mrs Brunty. The captain saw the child as a damned nuisance: he had enough problems getting his leaky old tub across the Irish Sea without having to concern himself with stowaways. But the cries of the child alarmed Mrs Brunty and brought her to see what was happening. From that point the captain had no alternative but to allow Mrs Brunty to do what she could for the boy until the ship reached Warrenpoint harbour. The discovery of the stowaway was entered in the ship's log, and after consulting his *Manual of Maritime Law*, the captain determined that the child should be handed to the port authorities in Warrenpoint. He was quick to notice, however, that Mrs Brunty had assumed absolute charge of the boy and would allow no-one near, during the passage, while she cleaned and cared for him. She told her husband and the captain that the boy was healthy, and suggested that his dark colouring was due to the fact that he was Welsh.

What was more likely than that he was born of a Welsh mother who for reasons unknown had given birth to the child in Liverpool? But the theory held no interest for the captain, who had already made up his mind on a course of action which would relieve him of any further responsibility in the matter.

At Warrenpoint he was courteous and calm, congratulating Mrs Brunty on her motherly handling of the child. As he was busy making ready for the unloading of his ship he suggested that she might carry the child ashore and talk to the port authorities about what had happened. She was happy to comply, but as she walked with the child down the gangplank on to Irish soil, the captain allowed himself a knowing smile.

Hugh Brunty was occupied with the unloading of some young stock he had bought in the market at Liverpool, so his wife walked alone with the child into the simple wooden hut which was the office of the harbourmaster. He received her kindly, listening impassively as she recounted the story of how the child had been discovered on the ship. Then he enquired what she intended to do with the child. She replied that she had done no more than any decent person would have done, but now felt that her responsibility in the matter was over. A rude shock awaited her. The harbourmaster pointed out that Warrenpoint had no facilities for caring for unwanted children. Further, he explained that a tax existed in Ireland for the carriage of illegitimate children to the nearest home for foundlings; the nearest such establishment was in Dublin. It was possible to make the necessary arrangements for the child to be taken there; but who was to pay the tax, and a token amount towards the welfare of the infant in the institution? The harbourmaster was adamant that his own office could not be expected to pay the money. The captain of the ship insisted, when sent for, that he had done his lawful duty to the owners of the ship in conveying the stowaway to the next port of call after discovery; beyond that he had no interest whatsoever. When Mrs Brunty suggested as a compromise that he might take the child back to Liverpool, where it had come from, the captain pointed out that that would be most irregular. It was obvious that someone had to come up with the money. Hugh Brunty was called for. He was understandably furious; angry with the captain; no less angry with the harbourmaster; but most of all angry with his wife. Had they not three children of their own? Why should Hugh Brunty of all people have to pay hard-earned money on account of a child who was no concern of his?

The argument raged for some time. Even when a local Minister of the Church was called in he could add nothing to the simple fact that someone – and it could not be himself – had to find the money. But who? Every participant in the argument had an excellent reason for not doing so. Finally the child's hungry cries were added to the bedlam, and at that Mrs Brunty made up her mind that the child would be taken home with them. Hugh Brunty stormed out of the hut, Mrs Brunty following him with the child. Hugh pleaded with her to put the boy out of her hands, but she would not budge. Her mind was made up. Since they could not pay the money, she reasoned, then the only thing to be done was to take the child to their own home and bring it up with the rest. Eventually, Hugh Brunty had to give in. By the time they had reached their home Mrs Brunty had given the child the name 'Welsh'.

And so a dark-haired, swarthy-skinned boy came to the Brunty home. The other children of the family were either fair or red-haired but they were told that the boy Welsh would always be regarded as their brother. His name was Welsh Brunty; and if the dark one was different from the rest he was never to be treated so.

Strangely, Hugh Brunty came to love Welsh more than any of his own. How that came about we shall see in the next story.

*   *   *

There were three children in the Brunty home at the time
Welsh was adopted, and at least two more were born later.
Accounts vary, and we must remember that we have no
means of discovering the certain truth. What we know comes
to us from the memories of people who heard the stories
from Hugh Brunty, the grandson of that Hugh Brunty who
adopted Welsh. There are no written records. But what
matters to the story is that Welsh was brought up as one of
the family, in which at least one of the children was younger
than himself. This was a girl called Mary, about whom we
shall hear more later.

For the moment we have Welsh along with the other
Brunty children, living as a family, and their father continuing his business as a cattle-dealer, making regular journeys
to and from Liverpool. The children squabbled as they do
in all families, and some have made a lot of this, suggesting that Welsh was forever causing trouble for the other
children, which perhaps he did, since he was the odd one out.
But as they grew older, Welsh was singled out from the rest,
because he had a way with cattle and horses, and loved the
whole business of cattle-dealing. Some people are born with
this special quality – a natural affinity with animals ; imp33-
ible to acquire – and Welsh was one of these people. The other
children had no interest at all in the cattle business. As a
result, Welsh and Hugh Brunty spent much of their time
together, and perhaps the other children resented this. When
their father went off to the fairs and markets in the surrounding area he took Welsh with him. Welsh helped Hugh with
the animals; and he soon became even more useful to his
adopted father in a way which is quite amusing in itself. At
the markets Welsh would leave Hugh and mingle with the
crowd, eavesdropping on groups of farmers who had brought
stock for sale. Being small, he was not noticed when prices
and qualities were being discussed outside the auction ring.
Scraps of information were carried to Hugh Brunty, and on
many an occasion it led to an astute bid at the right moment,

or to a shake of the head when he might have bought and
later rued it. As time went on, Hugh and Welsh formed a
close partnership. Anyone with knowledge of market trading
knows that there is a certain atmosphere in the markets, a
special quality of excitement which is what the business is
all about. Welsh revelled in it.

Going off early in the morning; travelling rough with the
animals; working hard all day around the auction ring;
returning home in the evening; discussing the successes and
the failures: all this was Welsh in his natural element. He
and his father became inseparable, and the partnership
prospered financially too. All the family reaped the benefits,
but it is not difficult to understand why the other Brunty
children were jealous. The boys in particular detested Welsh
and made no secret of it, except when their father was
present. No doubt Hugh often reminded them that they were
all living well out of the proceeds of their joint efforts. When
Hugh was not there, Welsh was perfectly capable of looking
after himself; although smaller than the other lads, he was
wiry and tough, and he was never afraid to fight. The other
dealers learned to respect him, because Welsh knew his business, and every year he grew more confident. He knew he
was not a Brunty by birth, nor by any legal document; but
by his own aptitude and hard work he stood by his father
as a loyal partner in the business which kept all the family
clothed and fed. Later, as a young man, he began to accom-
pany Hugh on the journeys to Liverpool. Before long he was
doing most of the work; as Hugh began to fail in health, so
young Welsh grew in stature and importance. Until the very
end, however, Hugh handled the money. Welsh resented this
at times, feeling that he should be trusted more; but whatever arguments were put forth, Hugh retained absolute control of the financial side of the business simply by never
allowing Welsh to handle the money. Welsh could do all the
dealing but, when it came to paying out, Hugh held the purse
strings. In this way he kept control. All accounts agree that

this single issue was the only point of dissension between the
two men.

One day Hugh and Welsh were returning from Liverpool
on the packet-boat to Warrenpoint after a successful time
in the market, when Hugh suffered a heart attack. He had
been ill on the trip over from Ireland, and had taken little
interest in the dealings at the market in Liverpool, apart
from handling the money. Welsh was attending the old man
when he died on board ship, and he accompanied the body
to the family home, where in the midst of the ensuing grief
it was discovered that there was very little money on the
body. There were no books either. Hugh had always kept
Welsh in complete ignorance about the money side of things,
and now who could say what had happened to the money
which should have been there? The brothers accused Welsh
of stealing it, and all the suppressed anger and resentment
which had built up over the years now burst out. The old
man lay dead, and there was no money. Welsh was tight-
lipped. The Brunty brothers told him that there was no
longer a place for him in the family home, and he was ordered
to leave. The widow and the daughters begged the brothers
not to do it, but their anger could not be appeased. Welsh
had never been legally adopted; he was not, in fact, a
Brunty. The boys with whom he had grown up were looking
at him now with hatred in their eyes, and there was nothing
to do but to leave without a fight. The man he had grown
to love as a father was dead in the room. Welsh was alone
in the world.

At this point, those familiar with the story of *Wuthering
Heights* will recognise the very clear similarity between this
tale of Welsh coming to the Brunty family, and that of
Heathcliff coming into the Earnshaw family. For those un-
familiar with Emily's novel, I submit a small passage from
Wuthering Heights which tells how Mr Earnshaw arrived
home with a great surprise for his family. This in no way

suggests plagiarism on the part of Emily Brontë. All writers write from within their own experience. They write from what they have seen, or heard, or felt, and I believe it is quite impossible to do otherwise. Nevertheless a writer, as distinct from a reporter, takes the information and sensation he has received, and creates from that the work of his imagination. I am sure that all the children of Patrick Brontë knew this story of Welsh being found on the boat from Liverpool, and this goes some way towards explaining a certain mystery about *Wuthering Heights*. There is some evidence that when the book was published, Branwell Brontë, Patrick's son who was addicted to drink and opium, declared in one of the inns he frequented that he had written the story himself. The evidence is confusing, and the witnesses are fairly unreliable, but certainly two men declared that they were present when Branwell said something of the kind. Perhaps Branwell said that he *could* have written it?

However, here is the passage from *Wuthering Heights* where a servant, Nellie Dean, is relating how her employer, Mr Earnshaw, arrived home after a business trip to Liverpool.

It seemed a long time to us all – the three days of his absence – and often did little Cathy ask when he would be home. Mrs Earnshaw expected him by supper-time, on the third evening, and she put off the meal hour by hour; but there were no signs of his coming however and at last the children got tired of running down to the gate to look. Then it grew dark; she would have had them to bed, but they begged sadly to be allowed to stay up; and, just about eleven o-clock, the door-latch was raised quietly, and in stepped the master. He threw himself into a chair, laughing and groaning, and bid them all stand off, for he was nearly killed – he would not have such another walk for the three kingdoms. 'And at the end of it, to be flighted to death!' he said, opening his great-coat, which he held bundled in his arms. 'See here, wife!, I was never so beaten with anything in my life: but you must e'en take it as a gift of God; though it's as dark almost as if it came from the devil.'

We crowded round, and over Miss Cathy's head I had a peep at a dirty, ragged, black-haired child; big enough both to walk and talk: indeed, its face looked older than Catherine's; yet, when it was set on its feet, it only stared round, and repeated over and over again some gibberish, that nobody could understand. I was frightened, and Mrs Earnshaw was ready to fling it out of doors: she did fly up, asking how he could fashion to bring that gypsy brat into the house, when they had their own bairns to feed and fend for? The master tried to explain the matter, but he was really half-dead with fatigue, and all that I could make out, amongst her scolding, was a tale of his seeing it starving, and houseless, and as good as dumb, in the streets of Liverpool; where he picked it up and inquired for its owner. Not a soul knew to whom it belonged, he said; and his money and time being both limited, he thought it best to take it home with him at once, than run into vain expense there: because he was determined he would not leave it as he found it. Well, the conclusion was that my mistress grumbled herself calm; and Mr Earnshaw told me to wash it, and give it clean things, and let it sleep with the children.

A few days after Hugh Brunty was buried the brothers received a message from Welsh. In it he stated that he had made a death-bed promise to their father, and he named a witness to the promise, a near neighbour who had been on the ship and had heard Hugh Brunty whisper his last few words to Welsh. The brothers consulted the neighbour, who confirmed that Hugh had indeed made a last request to Welsh, but although pressed to reveal what their father had said, the neighbour refused to speak about it. So a meeting was arranged. Welsh was asked to come to the house which had been his home, where the widow, her daughters, and her sons waited to hear what Hugh Brunty had requested before he died.

Welsh arrived, dressed as they had not seen him before, wearing a dark broadcloth suit, and a white linen shirt. He had taken some trouble to groom himself for the meeting, and his efforts did not go unnoticed by the family. There was something about his manner too, a confident and business-

like approach which was impressive. Welsh began to express
his sympathy, but a chilling reception dried up his words.
Quickly he moved on to telling about the last journey he
had made with Hugh. At one point Welsh was rudely inter-
rupted by one of the Brunty brothers crying out, 'tell us
what you did with the money!' But Welsh kept his temper
although he looked like thunder. Finally, he came to the
point, and told them that Hugh had asked him to promise
that he would stand by the family and run the business for
the benefit of all, because he, Hugh, loved him as a son. At
this the widow and the daughters were moved to tears, as
was Welsh himself. But the eldest of the brothers took this
moment to show the hatred he had felt for years. Making
no attempt to control his temper he told Welsh that he did
not believe a word of the story, and pointing to the table,
said that until the missing money was put on that table,
Welsh was not welcome in the home. Welsh was stung to
anger and he retorted that Hugh had given him complete
control because, as was patently obvious, he was the only
one of the family who could do what their father had done.
If the promise he had given to the man who had called him
a son was to be kept to the letter, he must have sole charge
of the family business. Welsh then told them of the heart-
break he had felt when coming home with the dead body
of the man he had loved, to be greeted by such mistrust and
hatred. They had ordered him from the only home he had
ever known. Yet he had given his promise, and that promise
would be kept if it was humanly possible. It was clear that
the brothers could not feel towards him as their father had
hoped, so there was only one solution: he would have to
become a legal member of the family. This suggestion was
met with silence. All, except one member of the family, were
wondering what Welsh could mean. They listened intently
as Welsh told them what he meant, in plain, simple words.
He looked directly across the table at Mary, the youngest
daughter, and firmly announced to the whole family that he

loved Mary, and wished to marry her. Mary was silent; her
face coloured with embarrassment. As her brothers shouted
their opposition to Welsh, Mary kept her eyes down. She
could not look at the man who had just said that he loved
her. Even when her mother took her arm and asked her to
speak, Mary could not. The eldest brother then took it upon
himself to speak for Mary, telling Welsh once again that his
presence was not wanted in the house. Welsh made one last
appeal to Mary, but she gave no sign of having heard him.
Only the anguished tears of Mrs Brunty prevented a fight
as the Brunty brothers moved in on Welsh, who stood with
fists clenched. The brothers were like panthers waiting to
pounce on him. Welsh backed slowly to the door. There, in
a white fury, he uttered these words, 'I swear to you all that
Mary will be my wife, and the day will come when this house
will be mine.' On that he turned and left the house. Mary
sat in her chair, her lips trembling, but no tears fell from
her staring eyes. Mrs Brunty wept openly while the brothers
looked at each other in impotent rage. Welsh's words hung
in the air. The double threat echoed in their ears. Each of
the brothers, in his own mind, knew that his hatred for Welsh
in that moment was enough to make him kill. Yet in their
hearts they knew they were afraid of him.

Welsh did not continue in the cattle business. Whatever his
reasons were he told them to no-one. The brothers made an
attempt to continue their father's business but it soon failed.
There was some sympathy for the lads in the market, but
it quickly dissipated when it became obvious that none of
them knew much about the trade. Within a year, two of the
Brunty brothers had gone to England, where they found
work which enabled them to send money home regularly.
The third brother went south, where he found employment
on a farm. He married and had children, but he died young;
we shall hear more about this brother and his family later
in the story.

As for Welsh, he found employment as a sub-agent in the business of estate management. The owner of the Brunty farm was an absentee landlord. Ireland was plagued with this system of land owned by rich men in England who cared little for their property except as a source of rent. The Bruntys lived in Ulster, which, broadly speaking, enjoyed a slightly higher standard of living than the rest of Ireland; but even in Ulster there was acute poverty. In Ulster also there was the problem caused by the ruthless 'planting' of Scottish and English protestants. Land was cheaply available to non-Catholic gentlemen who wished to acquire an estate. The Brunty family itself was never wealthy, but it is possible that they came to Ireland during the 'plantation' period in the seventeenth century. They were simply peasant farmers renting land from the owner of the estate, who lived in England. If he was like most of his kind he may never even have visited the country. The system was that the landowner appointed an agent to administer the estate, and that agent in turn appointed sub-agents who actually collected the rents. These sub-agents were empowered to raise the price of rents and to recommend eviction when they felt like it, and they were generally detested in consequence. The powers were, of course, often abused for personal reasons.

By becoming a sub-agent, Welsh placed himself in a position where he could keep a very interested eye on the Brunty farm, and report on its management. Presently he made it known to his employer that no men were living on the farm. The widow and the daughters were doing their best, and the rent was being paid, but Welsh offered a plan for the farm which would produce a better return for the landowner. This was music in the ear of the main agent.

In the meantime Welsh had secretly maintained his contact with Mary, and presently he made his move.

There lived in the area an old crone of a woman named Meg. Her surname is not known, but Meg was one of those

women often found living in rural areas who know everything and everybody. They prefer animals and wildlife to
people; but it is from people that the Megs of this world derive their greatest stimulation. For it is people who provide
the odd scrap of scandal and intrigue. The quarrel between
Welsh and the Brunty family was no secret, but very few
people knew that Welsh wanted Mary Brunty for his wife.
When Meg was told this she was only too happy to involve
herself. She became a frequent visitor to the Brunty home,
and, choosing her moments with consummate care, she let
Mary know that Welsh's interest in her had not waned. As
Welsh prospered as a sub-agent, Mary was kept closely informed of his progress, and of his desire that one fine day
he would be able to make her his wife.

When Mary heard from Meg that Welsh had something
of great importance to tell her; something far too private
to be passed on, even by Meg, it was a simple matter to
arrange a place and a time for a secret rendezvous. They met
in a copse near to Mary's home. She was afraid, but when
Welsh took her in his arms her fears left her. Soon Welsh
was telling her that she need have no more fears; his position
as a sub-agent was secure, and they could now marry. But
Mary was not willing to take the step which would cause such
distress and trouble with her family. She begged Welsh to
be patient a little while longer. Perhaps, she suggested, he
would come to the house and talk with her mother. But
Welsh had made up his mind. With Mary lying willingly in
his arms he was in no mood for talk of patience. Passionately
he told her that he loved her, and had loved her for years,
and now she was old enough to speak for herself without fear.
He promised Mary, as he had promised her father, that he
would never willingly act against the family interest. It was
more than enough to overcome Mary's reticence. Later,
when they lay together, Welsh told Mary that the physical
union would be made legal as soon as possible.

They were married in secret, but immediately afterwards

Welsh took his wife to the Brunty farm. Once the facts were known, and Welsh had stated that the house would be a home for Mrs Brunty and Mary's sister for as long as they wished to stay, all objections to the union melted away. For several months no problems arose. But in that time, Mary's brothers who were working away in England, received news of the marriage and returned to Ireland. The other brother in the south of Ireland took no interest.

When Welsh found himself confronted by the Brunty brothers, he warned them that an arrangement had been made with the agent, by which the farm was now rented to himself and Mary. The widow also pleaded with her sons to return to England, telling them that Welsh was a good hus band to their sister, and that the farm was all the better for having a man living there. But none of this interested the brothers. All they could see in Welsh was a man who had robbed them of family money, and was now robbing them of their home. They attacked Welsh in the house. He put up a good fight, but was receiving a sound beating when three of the agent's men burst into the room and overpowered the Brunty brothers. Welsh had taken the precaution of arranging for these men to be on hand if necessary,

The Brunty brothers were arraigned before the magis- trate, who was also the main agent in the area, and charged with trespass and assault. The magistrate pointed out that the man they had assaulted was the legal tenant of the farm. He was aware that it had once been their home, and they would have been welcomed there had their approach been reasonable and civilised. As it was, the courtesy of the tenant had been met with violence. The agent went on to speak of the farm itself. With only the widow and her daughters there, the farm had decreased in value. The rent had always been paid but there were other matters to consider besides paying the rent. From a strictly commercial point of view the farm could not be allowed to fall into a neglected condition, and Welsh was an experienced man, willing to accept the full responsibility. And he had done more: he had given the widow and the unmarried daughter a home for as long as they wished to take advantage of the generous offer. Finally the agent spoke of the landowner himself: the law must always protect the interest of property owners.

The Brunty brothers had taken the law into their own hands, at a time when lawlessness in Ireland had to be punished with the utmost severity for the benefit of all who lived there, so the brothers were sentenced to hard labour. It is thought that later they were transported to an overseas colony, for they were never heard of again. The date of the brothers' sentence is thought to be between 1750 and 1755.

Welsh was in his forties; Mary some ten years younger. No children were born to them. When next we hear of them, the widow and Mary's sister were not living on the farm. Possibly the daughter had married, and the widow was living with that daughter. What is known is that the brother who was living in the south of Ireland, died, leaving a widow and several children.

Chapter 3

Young Hugh's story

When Mary heard of her brother's death, she spoke to Welsh
about the possibility of adopting one of the children. Having
no child of her own, and reaching an age when it seemed unlikely that she might have one, Mary begged Welsh to offer
his help. No doubt she reminded him of his promise to stand
by the family. And so we hear of Welsh and Mary coming
to the home of her dead brother for the purpose of adopting
one of the children. It was never a legal adoption. This was
a family affair, common enough at the time, and the motiva-
tions are clear. For Mary, it meant a child of her own to love
and care for. For her sister-in-law it was one less child to
worry about. For Welsh it was an expression of his regard
for the man who had once adopted him. They chose the boy
called Hugh. All he knew was that he was going to live with
his aunt and uncle, and he went happily enough. Mary made
her sister vow never to try to contact her son again, nor ever
to reveal that she had given him up. It was agreed that for
the benefit of the boy, he should never know where his home
had been before he came to live with Welsh and Mary. The
boy grew up to become the father of ten children, one of them
Patrick Brontë, the father of the Brontë sisters. But the
boy's name was Hugh *Brunty*. All he ever remembered about
his adoption by Welsh and Mary was a long journey by horse
and cart, taking several days and nights. And he also

remembered that very soon after he arrived at his new home he was the subject of trouble between his new parents.

The trouble was over money. Welsh had been led to believe that a sum of fifty pounds would be forthcoming to help with the expense of having Hugh in the family. But the fifty pounds turned out to be five pounds. Soon after arriving in his new home, Hugh was told by Welsh that he would have to work for his living, though he was only seven, or possibly eight years old. It is clear that Welsh was a hard man who looked on the Bruntys as soft, lazy creatures. Welsh had had to struggle for himself as a boy, and there is plenty of reason in his attitude towards Hugh.

Besides Welsh, Mary, and Hugh, there was one other person living on the farm. This man, known only as Gallagher, was a servant in the house, who also helped Welsh in his business as sub-agent on the estate. Gallagher is described as a tall, gaunt man, fond of the drink, and sanctimonious to a degree. Always, when telling the tale of this part of his life, Hugh Brunty branded Gallagher as an utterly evil man who was nonetheless forever praising God and all the saints in heaven. For example, when Hugh was told by Welsh that he had been promised fifty pounds and had only been given five pounds, Gallagher was present. When Welsh left Hugh alone with Gallagher, the servant told him that, throughout his life, he would be punished for the sins of his mother. Hugh was told that all the saints in heaven would be against his happiness. To a very young boy the threat was terrifying; not unnaturally Hugh detested Gallagher from that moment.

As for Welsh, we are told that he was a bad-tempered man, heartily disliked in the area, and often involved in rows with his neighbours. His job as sub-agent alone would account for this. His attitude towards Hugh was unremittingly harsh. The boy was put to work on the farm, and was often beaten by Welsh. After every beating, Gallagher was there to remind the boy that he was being made to suffer for the sins of his mother. But there was another side to the coin. Soon after Hugh Brunty came to live with Welsh and Mary, the fortunes of Welsh took a decided downward plunge. It began when an agent was murdered. The killers were never discovered but the murder led to an enquiry. The landowner came over from England, and he was appalled at some of the tales told to him by his tenants. As a result Welsh lost his job, and soon after that disaster, another followed: the farmhouse was badly damaged by fire. Welsh swore that some of his neighbours were responsible, but nobody was ever charged with the offence, although the general opinion was that Welsh deserved all the bad luck which came his way. As a result Welsh had to spend a great deal of his time in rebuilding the ruined farmhouse, with no income apart from what the farm could produce.

These very changed circumstances would affect anyone, and it is possible that Welsh blamed the arrival of Hugh into his house, if not as the sole reason for the troubles, at least as the start of them. In any case, all we know about Welsh comes from Hugh Brunty. He certainly painted his uncle in very harsh colours, and without any redeeming feature; yet, and here is a mystery which I have not been able to solve in my own researches, Hugh Brunty came to name one of his own sons Welsh. In fact the name of Welsh seems to be a popular one in the family for it has appeared in almost every generation since. It seems odd that a man who was given such a villainous reputation by his biographer should be remembered by his name being given to new Bruntys through generations. Hugh Brunty himself gave the name Welsh to his own fifth son. Was it only that the name was given to a son born with dark hair, or was there in Hugh Brunty's mind some kind of love or respect for the man who treated him so harshly? The mystery must remain unsolved. None of the present generation of the family was able to suggest a reason to me, although they too had wondered why the name appears so often in the family.

It was in the company of his aunt Mary that Hugh found his only human friend in those years with Welsh. Mary was afraid of her husband, and when he was about, made no attempt to alleviate the slavish cruelty of Hugh's existence. But there were times when neither Welsh nor his crony, Gallagher, was on the farm, and on these rare but precious occasions Aunt Mary was able to succour her adopted son. It was from his aunt Mary that Hugh first heard that Welsh was not a true Brunty, and that he was not even a true Irishman! It is evident that the feelings she once had for her husband had grown sour over the years, and we can sense very strongly from Mary's relationship with Hugh that her own life was anything but happy.

Apart from Aunt Mary there was one great consolation in Hugh's life during these miserable years. It was a dog, a lean, long-backed, rough-haired dog of a yellowish colour. Very much a mongrel, it was the only dog on the farm and it took to Hugh as readily, and as warmly, as he took to it. The name of the dog was Keeper. Immediately we recall that the dog which Emily Brontë loved so much was also called Keeper. It is most unlikely that this is a coincidence. Presumably when Emily heard her father talking about *his* father, and the dog he had loved so much, the dog's name appealed, and when she had a dog of her own she chose the same name. Hugh Brunty always spoke lovingly of the dog which befriended him at a time when he was so alone. Many times he stated that but for the dog he would have died. Keeper always slept beside Hugh's bed. Through the day he went wherever the boy had to go: guarding cattle, gathering potatoes in the fields, working in the barn, or collecting wood and peat for the fires. For most of ten years the two were inseparable. Towards the end of his time with Welsh, his aunt Mary had turned to drink and was often out of her senses, so Hugh only had the company of Keeper to comfort him. He had no friends among the children of their neighbours, as they kept their children away from the unpopular Welsh. Finally it was a row between Welsh and a neighbour which directly led to Hugh's running away from home, when he was about sixteen years old.

The row between Welsh and his neighbour was over a piece of land. It was bogland, of small importance to either, but being adjacent to both properties, it led to a dispute over ownership. One day, the neighbour found Welsh on the disputed land. Hugh was witness to a fight between them, and saw Welsh take a beating. Afterwards he helped Welsh to get home, bruised and bleeding, and with the assistance of Gallagher, Welsh was put to bed. The next day Hugh was asked why he had not gone to Welsh's aid in the fight. Hugh replied that the fight was none of his affair, an attitude that angered Welsh. At the time he felt too weak to punish Hugh, but he swore that he would beat him as soon as he could get out of his bed. For the next few days Gallagher gloated over the punishment that was to be meted out. On every possible opportunity he taunted Hugh and on one ocasion too many, for the lad lost his temper. Gallagher was no match for a strong young man. The fight was short-lived, and ended with Gallagher running away back to the farm to tell his master. On impulse, Hugh decided to run away, and he left with nothing. Even the dog, Keeper, was left behind out of fear that he would be recognised all too easily. Hugh ran for miles, crying from fear and desperation, and coming to a river, swam across it. On the far bank he permitted himself one last look back. But even for his aunt Mary there was nothing left but pity.

He travelled on, and after a night spent in a hayrick, made another day's journey. Coming to the town of Carlingford, he passed quickly through as he thought Welsh might have tried to find him. A few miles further on Hugh came to some lime-kilns, owned at that time by a company known as Swift McNeill's. There he found refuge. The owners needed labour, so Hugh applied and was accepted with no questions asked. He was given a place to sleep, and after a couple of days

he found a good lodging. He could read and write, thanks
to his aunt Mary, and had a head for simple arithmetic. These
qualities, added to his ability to work hard, and a cheerful
disposition, led to success in the lime-kilns. Within a year
he was an overseer, with the special responsibility of dealing
with the farmers who came to buy lime.

As far as Hugh knew, Welsh made no attempt to find out
where he had gone, and from the moment that he began at
Swift McNeill's, he put the past completely behind him. His
employers never asked where he had come from, and Hugh
never saw or heard of Welsh again. He was alone in the world,
but he was strong and happy with his new life. If ever a
young man wiped the slate clean and started again, that man
was Hugh Brunty. And he always said that his only regret
in life was in not taking his dog, Keeper, with him.

There are few of us who have never, at some time in our
youth, wanted to run away. Whatever our background, and
however comfortable or otherwise the home may be, it is
quite commonplace for us to have the urge to strike out on
our own. But of the many who think of it only a few actually
do it; and of those, a great many return very quickly. After
all, it is an enormous undertaking for a young person. For
Hugh Brunty it must have been a great emotional shock,
and one he would never forget. His home with Welsh and
Mary was not a happy one but, although Welsh was undoubtedly a hard man, there is in Hugh's stories some sort
of respect and understanding for Welsh. He is described as
a brute but we are led to believe that it was life that made
him so. Aunt Mary was a weak person and a hopeless alco-
holic, but she was kind, and we feel sorry for her. Gallagher
was all bad.

It is worthwhile to consider the pictures of these people
given to us by Hugh. For although he ran away from them,
in one sense he took them with him. All his life Hugh Brunty
hated injustice, hypocrisy, and weakness. He became an out-

spoken man in a time when to speak out against the injustices in Ireland was very dangerous indeed. Hugh was neither Catholic nor Protestant, so he spoke out against both religions because, to his mind, they were equally guilty of teaching hatred against the other. He also spoke out against the laws of the land, because he believed that Ireland should be governed by Irishmen. Most of all he attacked, openly and often, the laws which related to tenancy. As we shall see, Hugh Brunty became a revolutionary, but with words, not weapons. Many people thought that he was mad, and perhaps this saved his life, for he joined no party, and throughout his life he remained a simple man who entertained with his gift of story-telling. There were social, religious, and political undertones to all his stories; but his gift made the stories into entertainment, and he was never regarded as anything more than a 'character'.

But all this lies ahead. First we must see what happened to him at the Swift McNeill lime-kilns. He arrived there barely sixteen, absolutely penniless and unknown. But his personality made him popular with his employers and their customers, which, in turn, led to promotion and success. Farmers came to the lime-kilns from a wide surrounding area. One of his customers, who came regularly from County Down, was Patrick McClory, a red-haired lad of about Hugh's age, and a friendship was struck up between them. Patrick McClory, who was known as Red Paddy McClory, lived near the village of Ballynaskeagh, about eight miles north-east of Newry. Over the course of a couple of years the friendship deepened. Hugh told Red Paddy the story of his life with Welsh and Mary; Red Paddy told Hugh that his own parents were dead, and that he farmed in a small way with his sister to help him. Paddy McClory was a Catholic, but this was of no consequence to the two lads at this stage of their lives. When Red Paddy came for lime, he took to staying the odd night with Hugh, and before long Red Paddy was suggesting that Hugh should come up to Ballynaskeagh for a visit. The

friendship was very firm indeed, and it was to survive
stresses which would have broken anything less. One year,
as Christmas approached, Red Paddy insisted that his friend
should take advantage of the few days' holiday and come
to see his farm. He was concerned that Hugh would be spending Christmas alone, and Hugh accepted the offer. By this
time Hugh was a confident young man. His wages were more
than enough to supply his needs; he could afford good
clothes, and he had money to jingle in his pockets. In due
course he set out for Newry, and there he hired a rig, in which
he rode up to the McClory cottage on Christmas Eve. He
was feeling on top of the world. In just a few years the runaway boy had become a handsome young man, and he was
going to spend Christmas with the closest friend he had ever
known.

The McClory cottage in Ballynaskeagh still stands today,
in a rural setting not very different from that Christmas Eve
when Hugh Brunty rode up to it, and it is not difficult to
imagine the scene. Today the road is tarmacadamed, and the
cottage is not lived in, but the glen faces the front door, and
there is little to remind one of the twentieth century. When
Hugh Brunty pulled up outside the cottage and walked to
the door he had not the slightest intimation that he was
about to have one of the greatest surprises of his life. A young
girl opened the door to his knock. She was tall, about sixteen
or seventeen years old, with long, golden hair hanging to her
shoulders in ringlets. Her eyes were a deep hazel, framed with
long dark eyelashes, common amongst Irish beauties. She
was proud too, and filled with the joy of living. It was said
by many that no prettier girl existed in County Down, and
she knew it. Alice was the sister of Red Paddy McClory. She
smiled a welcome to the young man about whom she had
heard so much from her brother. Hugh instantly fell head
over heels in love. He said of the moment that he was completely stunned by the beauty of the girl who stood before
him. So much so that he stammered when he tried to speak.

When Alice turned, and beckoned Hugh to enter, he clumsily banged his head on the door frame. Alice laughed as their eyes met. It was a case of love at first sight, often written about but rarely experienced. The two would eventually marry, but the road ahead was to prove very thorny indeed.

It was about the year 1774 when Hugh Brunty met Alice McClory. These were times when travel of any kind was difficult; consequently people lived in close, tight communities, and a stranger was always suspect. Though Hugh was an amiable young man, and he came to Ballynaskeagh as a friend of Red Paddy McClory, he was still a stranger about whom very little was known. However, for a few days the spirit of Christmas prevailed. The McClory home was visited by many local friends and relatives, and Hugh was caught up in the celebrations of goodwill to all men. He declined to attend Mass on Christmas Day but no importance was attached to his refusal. Hugh spent as much time as possible in the company of Alice. It soon became clear to Red Paddy that his friend had fallen in love with Alice, and that his sister had taken to the handsome young stranger. During the holiday Red Paddy taught Hugh how to handle a firearm and the two of them went out hunting for small game. On one of these occasions, Hugh told his friend that he was in love. To Red Paddy this was the best of news. Later in the day Alice confessed that she returned Hugh's affection; and before the holiday was over she told Red Paddy that Hugh had asked her to marry him. Hugh was a passionate man, not the sort to be cautious when in love, and we shall see in time that his son, Patrick, was of the same temperament. As soon as Red Paddy made the announcement to his family, the spirit of Christmas faded away. Hugh, Alice, and Red Paddy were all young, and the young are almost always considered to be foolish, especially when there is talk of love.

Troops of relatives and family friends now arrived at the McClory house, and every one of the same mind: there could never be a marriage between Alice and a Protestant. It was out of the question. The Catholics and the Protestants were divided in Ireland, as much then as they are now, and the two religions had already become rallying flags for militants. Although the true reasons for the discord lie in the areas of race, land ownership, and equal rights, it is under the banners of religion that the battles were, and still are, fought. The twelfth of July is a day to drink to the victory of King William at the battle of the Boyne. The seventeenth of March is for the other side to drink to St Patrick, and to curse King William. If this seems bizarre today, it appeared no less so to young Hugh Brunty, who had never been in a church of any denomination in his life. But to the McClory clan, and they were numerous and vociferous, it was unthinkable that their lovely Alice should marry such a man. Hugh prepared to meet them, sure in his own mind that love would prevail. He assured Alice and Red Paddy that he had the simple answer to all their problems. Since he was neither Catholic nor Protestant, what objection could there be? He would tell them all that he loved Alice McClory, and that she loved him. Alice had accepted his proposal of marriage, and he intended to make the necessary arrangements as soon as possible for a wedding to which all would be welcome. No doubt Hugh lay awake the night before the meeting, thinking of how he was going to put his arguments to the McClorys. The story which Hugh told about that meeting is an amusing one; but when it actually happened, it must have seemed a nightmare end to all his dreams.

When the relatives and friends arrived at the McClory house they were shown into the kitchen, where Alice had prepared food. Her brother, Red Paddy, had prepared for other needs: whiskey, and plenty of it. For a while the guests were only too happy to eat and drink, and no-one seemed in a hurry to make the first move, but finally one of the relatives asked in a kindly manner if Hugh would care to speak his mind. Hugh obliged. When someone then asked Hugh why he was not drinking with the company, Hugh replied that he detested the stuff. The atmosphere in the room cooled noticeably. Another relative raised the religious question. Was Hugh prepared to abandon his Protestant faith? Hugh replied that he was not of the Protestant conviction. To a further question as to whether he had considered the idea of becoming a Catholic, Hugh replied that he had indeed, and the answer was a straightforward 'no'. 'What about the possible outcome of the proposed union?' someone called out. 'If you mean what about children,' replied Hugh, 'I hope we have many, and I will leave it to Alice to decide whether they are brought up Catholic or Protestant, for to be honest with you I don't give a damn either way.' This was Hugh's trump card on which he had based his hopes. The idea had come to him in the middle of a sleepless night, and he had banked on it. Unfortunately it was a certain loser. A fiery little man who had been taking his share and a bit more of the whiskey, got to his feet, and enforced his question with a mighty thump on the table. 'But will you curse King William?' Hugh was unwise enough to laugh at the question. Others now leaped to their feet, all demanding if Hugh was prepared to curse King William. Hugh raised his arms to ask for order. Then, calmly and carefully he said, 'I will not curse any man whom I do not know.' At this, one of the relatives who had hitherto said nothing at all, but had taken a very sociable share of the whiskey, rose on unsteady legs to demand, 'Then tell us your opinion of the Pope!' Unfortunately the question came at a time when Hugh's temper had risen beyond the danger level. His reply was unwise, but honest, and delivered with some force. 'If he is the head of a religion which calls for people to curse a man who's been dead for years, then I reckon he could do with a cursing himself!' It was the end of what might be called the discussion, and the beginning of what can only be called a riot. A fist struck Hugh, and he replied by picking up his chair and cracking it down hard on the heads of the nearest of his attackers. Owing to the amount of whiskey which had been consumed, the fight was very disorderly from the beginning, and rapidly developed into chaos. Nobody was sure who was fighting whom, and in the general confusion Hugh managed to get out of the room. In fact he had been gone from the house for half an hour before Red Paddy was able to stop the fight. Later that night, when most of the belligerents were sleeping it off, Hugh met Alice in secret before he left the village. He promised her that the love they had would never be blighted by time or distance; and that, somehow, he would overcome all the obstacles that now lay between them. Alice promised herself again, and swore that nothing would ever change her mind. Red Paddy who, during the fight had been seen striking out at anyone who came near him, kept out of things. These people were his relatives and friends, and he had to live with them. All he could offer his friend was the advice to clear out for a while and let things cool down. But it seemed to Hugh and Alice, as they kissed goodbye that night, that the whole McClory family would never accept their marriage. The future looked very bleak, but as in all Brontë, or Brunty, stories, a little hardship was no deterrent to true love.

Chapter 4

Hugh and Alice

Hugh returned to his work at the lime-kilns near Carlingford, only a shade over ten miles, from the village of Ballynaskeagh. It was a journey that Hugh Brunty came to know very well. The lovers met many times over the course of a year, always in secret, although it is very likely that Red Paddy knew about the meetings. There is a glen near the McClory cottage which is today known as the 'lovers' arbour'. Local legend has it that this was one of the places where Hugh and Alice used to meet.

These trysts were always on a Sunday, when Hugh could leave the kilns. Soon, however, his employers noticed that Hugh's mind was not as firmly directed towards his work as it had been, giving cause for complaint. Also at this time, Hugh became somewhat less friendly and cheerful than he had been in the past. He was often found studying the Bible, but it is more likely he was trying to improve his skills at reading and writing, than grappling with the mysteries of religion. Letters passed between Hugh and Alice, possibly with the help of Red Paddy. However, when one of these letters was discovered by another member of the family, Red Paddy joined with the rest in suggesting that the love affair should end. There seemed to be no future in the romance. Hugh had very little money; his work was suffering from his distraction; the hostility towards him was, if anything, on

the increase; and both Alice and Hugh were very unhappy.
Red Paddy begged both of them to be sensible. The only
outcome of all this was that the lovers became even more
secretive. Red Paddy was led to believe that the affair had
died a natural death.

More complaints about Hugh's work compelled his
employers to speak to him, but there was no improvement,
and finally Hugh was given the sack. Out of a job, and out
of his lodgings, Hugh went to the nearby town of Newry,
where there was a hiring ground for labour on the market.
He was engaged by James Harshaw, a gentleman who owned
land near Donoughmore, which is only two or three miles
from Ballynaskeagh. We can sense the will of Hugh at this
time in his life. Obviously he was completely unconcerned
as to what he did for a living, as long as he could do it near
to the woman he loved. At the Harshaw house, Hugh was
treated very well. Although hired as a farm labourer he soon
became a house-servant, and much of his time was spent with
the children of the Harshaws. Being so close to where Alice
lived, Hugh had no difficulty in arranging to see her very
often, usually in the glen, but Alice had a mare of her own,
and she made it her business secretly to ride to wherever
Hugh was working.

A local farmer, also fond of horse-riding, began to take
an interest in Alice. It was natural that the two should meet
whilst exercising their horses, and the relationship grew
steadily. His name was Joe Burns – a Catholic, and a well-
respected man in Ballynaskeagh. Alice appeared to be
pleased by the man's attentions; Red Paddy knew him well;
and the whole McClory clan approved of him. Their friendship soon became the talk of the village. Such a pretty girl
as Alice deserved a fine husband like Joe. As to Alice's be-
haviour throughout this courtship, there can be no doubt
that she was willing. Finally to everyone's delight, it was
announced that the couple were engaged to be married. Alice
entered into all the excitement and the arrangements with-

out a sign of duplicity. Possibly she was trying to convince herself that she could grow to love Joe Burns. The wedding day was fixed for the summer of 1776. The local dressmaker was hired to make the wedding dress, while Joe made all the arrangements for a huge feast, to which all the village were invited. With Joe being short of neither money nor friends, the celebration looked like being a really grand affair, and the excitement caught the attention of a great many people. Away from Ireland there was news of a revolution in the American colonies, but what was that compared to the planning of a village wedding and an open feast. Not only the interest, but the skills of a great many people were involved. Joe Burns wanted everyone to enjoy the great day. Finally, when the day dawned, everyone could see that it was going to be a glorious summer day. The gods were smiling.

In the McClory house, Alice had stayed up, making last-minute alterations to her dress. Red Paddy rose early. There was plenty for him to do so he left Alice undisturbed. One of the customs in the area at the time involved a horse race to the home of the bride-to-be, so the bridegroom and his friends met early, about a mile from the McClory house. That morning, the horses were as excited as their riders. The race to the home of the bride-to-be was on. The winner of the race – if that it could be called, for it was more a cavalry charge than a race – would receive 'the broth', which meant a kiss from Alice McClory, the most beautiful girl in County Down. Joe Burns was intending that no-one but himself would claim that particular prize! A crowd of neighbours had taken up position to watch the race, and a great shout went up as the race started and the cavalcade came thundering down the hill towards the McClory cottage. Several riders lost their seats, but right at the head of the charge was Joe Burns on his huge black horse. Red Paddy was at the door of the cottage to greet him and there followed an awkward pause for the company while Red Paddy and Joe Burns talked in private. Apparently Alice had gone out early on her mare,

and had not returned. The horsemen immediately separated
into groups to search for Alice in case an accident had
befallen her. However, someone arriving for the wedding
reported that Alice had been seen on her mare, accompanied
by another man on a horse. The pair had been seen galloping
towards the river Bann near Banbridge.

Whilst this piece of information was being discussed, a
young boy rode up on Alice's mare. He carried two written
messages, one for Joe Burns, the other for Red Paddy. Both
contained the same news! Alice McClory had married Hugh
Brunty in the church at Magherally. It was a Protestant
church, a few miles out of Banbridge, and at the time, the
vicar was a friend of the Harshaw family. In the letters Alice
begged to be forgiven. She said that at the very last minute
she had decided that she could not go through with the wedding to Joe Burns, although she liked and respected him.
She had met with Hugh Brunty, and together they had decided that their love for each other could not be denied. Finally Alice asked that the feast should not be spoiled on
account of her. She called for her family and friends to drink
her health as Mrs Hugh Brunty, which was what she was,
and what she wanted to be. To the great credit of Joe Burns,
he read out his letter to the assembled crowd who were waiting to hear what had happened. Joe declared that he was
not the man to stand in the way of such a love; and taking
up his glass he proposed a toast to Alice and her chosen husband. Red Paddy took it from there, raising his glass and
shaking the hand of his friend. Then Joe announced that a
lot of time and trouble had been spent on preparing a feast
that the people of Ballynaskeagh would never forget. Would
it not be a crime to let the food and drink go begging? After
all Alice was married, which was half of the reason for the
feast, and as for himself, why, this left him free to see what
else was about!

Joe Burns was a fine man. His personality carried the day
and the feast was celebrated. By the end of the day, even

those remaining sober bore no grudge against Hugh and Alice. Red Paddy and Joe Burns both stated that the couple would be made welcome in Ballynaskeagh if they chose to make their home there. The grandfather of the Brontë sisters had found his bride. From the moment Alice became Mrs Brunty she demonstrated that her beauty was matched by her determination and resourcefulness. It was a union based firmly on love, and with strong character on both sides, as we shall see.

The church at Magherally is now a ruin, but the outcome of the wedding celebrated there on that summer's morning in 1776 was quite remarkable.

There is no record we can look at to verify the wedding of Hugh and Alice. All we know is that they married in the early summer of 1776, at Magherally Church. Today the church has no roof, but there is enough of the building left standing for us to be able to picture quite clearly what it looked like at the time. If the lost records are ever found it is most probable that the names will read Hugh Brunty and Elinor McClory, for that is how the couple were named in registers dating from 1779. The name of Hugh's wife is spelled as Elinor or Eleanor: the name Alice is never recorded although she was always known by that name. Because of Hugh, it was not possible for them to be married in a Catholic church, and because they were not married in a Catholic church, they were not regarded by Catholics as being 'lawfully' wed, although they certainly were. The fact that they came from different religious backgrounds had an effect on their children, as we shall see.

Immediately after the ceremony the couple went to Warrenpoint for a short holiday. The journey of eighteen or so miles would have taken a few hours. According to Hugh they travelled in a carriage, carefully avoiding the area of Ballynaskeagh by taking the road through Rathfriland. Hugh knew the town of Warrenpoint very well. It lies across the Carlingford Lough from the lime-kilns where he had worked

for several years. No doubt Hugh had friends in Warrenpoint
and had selected a suitable lodging for the honeymoon. For
a week they spent their time walking along the banks of the
lough, enjoying each other's company, and no doubt discussing the future. The lough provides a good harbour for sailing-
ships, and it would have been full of them. It is protected
from all winds except from the south-east, and is a lovely,
natural harbour surrounded by mountains. Perhaps the
packet-boat from Liverpool came in to the harbour while
Hugh and Alice were there. If so, no doubt Hugh took the
opportunity to tell Alice how the man who had adopted him
had been found abandoned on the boat.

Before the end of the holiday they had a visit from Red
Paddy McClory. He came to tell them that they would be
welcome in Ballynaskeagh, and that Joe Burns bore them
no grudge. A marriage kept secret from relations and friends
is a very serious affair. There is no knowing what the effect
on those people will be; and although the excitement of the
drama tends for a time to obscure reality, the simple facts
of life very quickly bring the romantics down to earth. The
problem most pressing on Hugh and Alice was simply how
and where could they best make their life together. Hugh
had agreed to return to his employment with the Harshaws
at Donoughmore, who had always treated him kindly. There
was no reason now to desert them without serving a reasonable notice, especially as it was summer and the harvest season about to begin, so Red Paddy came up with a sensible
suggestion. His sister Alice could return to the family home
for a time, and Hugh would always be a welcomed visitor.
Hugh could help to bring in the harvest for the Harshaws,
and in the meantime everyone would keep their eyes open
for a home for the pair of them. If the couple were prepared
to consider living in the Ballynaskeagh area, then Red
Paddy was sure that a home would be found quite soon. All
this was agreed upon at Warrenpoint, and after the honeymoon the bride returned to the McClory cottage at Ballynas-

keagh, while Hugh worked the harvest for his employer at Donoughmore, and went regularly to see his new wife. Hugh and Alice were a popular couple, and now they were married it didn't seem to matter that one was Catholic and the other not. In September Alice knew for sure that she was expecting a child, making the search for a home more urgent. Eventually one was found, less than a mile from the McClory cottage, in a village called Imdel or Emdale. The two spellings are used even today. The rent of the cottage was offered at sixpence a week, payable by the normal custom of one day's work a week for the landowner. It was a very small cottage, but it was convenient, and the couple moved in before the winter began. The child growing inside Alice would be born there, the child who would become the father of the Brontë sisters, and no simpler birthplace could be imagined than the cottage at Imdel. The ruins of the first home of the parents of Patrick Brontë can be seen today.

By today's standards the cottage at Imdel would not be classed as a house at all. In fact it was a single-storey building of rough stone with a thatch roof, divided into two small rooms. Access from the road outside was through a wooden door into the living-room, in which there was a chimney recess. The rear room was used as a bedroom. The floors were of earth, covered in straw or dry reeds. There were, of course, no toilet facilities, nor was there a water supply to the cottage, but in these respects the cottage differed in no way from most of the homes in Ballynaskeagh. In the census of 1841, taken sixty-five years after Hugh and Alice moved into their home at Imdel, it was recorded that nearly half the families of the rural population of Ireland were living in one-roomed, windowless mud cabins. Conditions in Ulster were considerably better than in the rest of Ireland, so Hugh and Alice no doubt considered themselves fortunate.

Working on the Harshaw estate, Hugh Brunty had learned the skills of an agricultural labourer. There were, however, very few estates or farms requiring the full-time services of an agricultural labourer. For several reasons but mostly because of the rapid increase in the population, the land had been split into smaller and smaller holdings, to the point where each family had its own portion of land, known as a 'sod', and they were able to manage this without any help. The Devon Commission reported in 1845, after a two-year enquiry into the conditions prevailing in Ireland, that the general living standards of the peasants were amongst the lowest in Europe. Bearing in mind that this enquiry was made almost seventy years after Hugh and Alice took the cottage at Imdel, it gives us some indication of the sort of community in which they were hoping to make a living. They had found a home, and were not without friends. A 'sod' of land was provided by Red Paddy McClory on which the Bruntys could grow their own potatoes, and on this frugal basis they began their married life. Before very long, Hugh had thought of an idea which arose directly from his earlier experiences at Carlingford, and was to become his main occupation for many years. He constructed a simple kiln in the fireplace of the cottage at Imdel, for the drying of corn. One of the chief differences between the standard of life in Ulster and that in the rest of Ireland, was that in Ulster the basic diet of potatoes was augmented by growing corn. The villagers of Ballynaskeagh grew their corn, did their best to dry it in the sun, and then took the corn to the miller for grinding into meal. Hugh offered them a useful service. His kiln would dry the corn more efficiently, and would operate twenty-four hours a day. For payment, Hugh extracted a small portion of corn from every sack to be dried. The idea soon caught on, and before long Hugh was drying corn not only for his neighbours but for people all over the county. In the evenings, Hugh's fireplace became a gathering point for the men of the village. Whilst the evening meal was being cooked in their own homes the men liked to gather around Hugh's glowing fire. It was here that Hugh earned his reputation as a story-teller. Illuminated by the light from the fire, and warmed by the heat of it, Hugh's audiences grew until he became known over a wide area as a great talker. He had 'the gift'. It is a talent well respected in Ireland, not to be confused with 'blarney', which is nothing more than deceiving; a man who has 'the gift' is one who can tell a story well. Hugh Brunty had the talent to such a marked degree that his fame lived on long after he had died. Even at the end of the nineteenth century, when Dr William Wright was researching for his book, *The Brontës in Ireland*, he found many people were able to recall what *their fathers* had heard around the fire in Hugh's cottage.

As Hugh was building his reputation as a corn-drier and story-teller, so his young wife, Alice, was making an equal reputation as a spinner and weaver of wool. Alice could take the raw wool from the sheep, card, spin, and dye it, and then weave or knit the yarn into finished garments. These home-spun clothes were worn by all the family. Their first child, Patrick, preferred wool to any other material, and he carried this preference with him throughout his long life.

We are at the end of one part of the story, with Hugh married to Alice, and their first child about to appear. Up to this point, to a very large degree, we have had to accept Hugh Brunty's version of his early life, and how he came to marry Alice McClory. We cannot be sure when he was born or where, as births were not compulsorily registered in Ireland until 1863, and although church records were kept, many were destroyed. We have only Hugh's word for the story of how he came to be adopted by Welsh Brunty, and for what we know about Welsh himself. It is doubtful if the whole tale is pure invention; but it must be equally doubtful if the tale is wholly true. It was told many times over and we know of it only by hearsay. The bulk of this comes to us by virtue of the work done by Dr William Wright when he was compiling his book, from 1890 to 1893. At that time he interviewed many people who knew the Brunty family, including church ministers and old residents living in the area, who had heard about Hugh and his tales from their parents, who were contemporaries of Hugh's. In 1891 Miss Ellen Nussey, a personal friend of Charlotte Brontë, paid a visit to the home of Dr Wright, and he tells us she was able to help him. Unfortunately the one man who could have told so much about Hugh Brunty was his firstborn son; and Patrick, for whatever reasons, said very little about his father. Mrs Gaskell must have tried with all her skill as a writer to find out more about Hugh Brunty, and about the family origins in Ireland. We know from the results of her labours that she found out precious little. Patrick told her only what he wanted her to know. As far as he was concerned the Brontë genius began with himself. Over his own background he preferred biographers to leave the curtain drawn. Mr J. A. Erskine-Stuart wrote a biography of Patrick's family in Haworth after they were all dead, and in his book we can read, 'For our own part, we desire a fuller biography of the family than has yet been written, and we trust, and are confident, that such will yet appear, and that there are many surprises yet in store for students of this Celtic circle.' The Reverend Patrick Brontë took his silence with him to the grave. All we are left with are the tales told by his father, which may or may not be true, and are in any case only memories of the man. But we need not be dismayed, for Patrick never quite managed to draw the curtain completely. In the closeness of his own family circle, around the fireside in the parsonage at Haworth, Patrick told his children the tales his father had told him. We must remember that Patrick was quite a story-teller. He knew how to take an audience by the throat and shake it. We know, for instance, that the girls often had sleepless nights after listening to Patrick's tales. And we know more. The story of how Welsh Brunty came to be abandoned by his mother on that ship in Liverpool harbour ... how he was resented by the children he grew up with ... and how he fought with them in later years ... all this is so similar to the story in *Wuther-*

ing Heights that we cannot conceive it to be a coincidence. Then there is the dog which Hugh befriended on Welsh's farm. The name was Keeper. Emily Brontë had a dog she loved dearly. His name was Keeper. The character of Gallagher is surely the model on which Emily Brontë built her character of Joseph, the servant in *Wuthering Heights*. Above all there is the fact that all the Brontë sisters wanted desperately to entertain by telling stories – as their father did – and as *his* father did. The formula for success in this field is a simple one. Take life and tell about it in such a way that emotion is imprinted forever on the mind of the listener. That is the magic of the Brontë genius.

Hugh is thought to have written a poem at the time when he and Alice lived in the cottage at Imdel. The poem was later edited by his son Patrick.

Alice and Hugh

The red rose paled before the blush
That mantled o'er thy dimpled cheek;
The Peach-bloom faded at the flush
That tinged thy beauty ripe and meek.

Thy milk-white brow outshone the snow,
Thy lustrous eyes outglanced the stars;
Thy cherry lips, with love aglow,
Burned ruddier than the blood-red Mars.

Thy sweet, low voice waked in my heart
Dead memories of my mother's love;
My long-lost sister's artless art
Lived in thy smiles, my gentle dove.

Dear Alice, how thy charm and grace
Kindled my dull and stagnant life!
From first I saw thy winning face
My whole heart claimed thee for my wife.

I thought you'd make me happy, dear,
I sought you for my very own;
You clung to me through storm and fear,
You loved me still, though poor and lone.

My love was centred all in self,
Thy love was centred all in me;
True wife above all pride and pelf,
My life's deep current flows for thee.

The finest fibres of my soul
Entwine with thine in love's strong fold,
Our tin cup is a golden bowl,
Love fills our cot with wealth untold.

It is a passionate poem, whatever else may be said about it, written by a passionate man, and we will see that his son, Patrick, was no less so. All the Brontë children had the same characteristic. From the first line of the last verse of the poem we can trace an echo which appears in the story of *Jane Eyre*. When Rochester asks Jane if she is suited by him, Jane replies, 'To the finest fibres of my nature, Sir.' Charlotte evidently knew the poem 'Alice and Hugh'.

The seventeenth of March is celebrated as St Patrick's Day. The firstborn child to Hugh and Alice Brunty was born on St Patrick's Day in the year 1777. As we have already observed, the church register which contained the entry for Patrick's baptism has been lost, and we have only the register dating from 1779. There is every reason to believe that the entry concerning Patrick would be similar to that concerning the next child to be born to the Bruntys, William, and if the lost page is ever found it will probably read: 17 March 1777. Patrick, son of Hugh and Elinor Brunty, Drumballyroney.

In that year of 1777, St Patrick's Day would have been celebrated as a holiday in Ireland; and in the tiny cottage at Imdel there was a very special reason to celebrate the day.

No doubt the cottage was visited by many neighbours wanting to congratulate Hugh and Alice on the birth of their first child, and a son at that. Patrick Brunty was alive and very well.

Chapter 5

The young Patrick

By the end of the year 1779, the little cottage at Imdel was
proving to be too small for the Brunty family. Patrick was
in his third year, and his brother William, almost a year old.
William was christened on 16 March in the nearby church
at Drumballyroney where Patrick had also been christened.
The two little boys slept with their parents in the back room
of the cottage; the front room being used as a living- and
dining-room, with Hugh's corn-drying kiln in one corner.
Aside from looking after her growing family, Alice was
always busy spinning and weaving the wool taken from
sheep on her brother's farm. Clearly the marriage of Hugh
and Alice was proving to be successful, and despite the circumstances of their elopement the couple were totally
accepted and integrated into the local community. Hugh and
Alice were content, despite their low income and tiny home.
By the standards of today their diet would be considered
dreary and insufficient to maintain health, but the Bruntys,
and millions like them, thrived on it. In Dr William Wright's
book, *The Brontës in Ireland*, there is a fine description of
life for an Irish peasant in those days.

The land of the thriftless brought forth potatoes in plenty. A
little lime and dyke scourings mixed together sufficed for manure.
The potato seed was planted on the lea-sod, and covered up in

ridges four or five feet wide. The elaborate preparation for planting potatoes in drills was then unheard of. Cabbage plants were dibbled into the edges of the ridges, and the potatoes and cabbages grew together. Abundant supplies of west-reds and yellow-legs and copper-duns, with large savoy and drumhead cabbages, only needed to be dug and gathered to maintain existence.

Oats, following the potato crop, provided rough, wholesome bread, and little rats of Kerry cows supplied milk. Great, stalwart men and women lived on potatoes three times a day, with bread and buttermilk and an occasional egg. Sometimes in the autumn a lean and venerable cow would be fed for a few weeks on the after-grass (flesh put on in a hurry being considered more tender), and then killed, salted, and hung up to the black balk in the kitchen for family use. This pièce de résistance was almost the only meat ever known in the homes of such people. The wool of the sheep, spun and knitted and woven at home, supplied scant but sufficient wardrobes. For fuel they had whins, or furze, cut from the fences and turf from the bogs. The fire was preserved by raking a half-burnt turf every night in the ashes; but a coal to light the fire was occasionally borrowed in the morning from more provident neighbours, and carried with a pair of tongs from house to house. Matches were unknown in those days.

The men broke stones by the roadsides on warm days for pocket money or tobacco, and the women obtained their little extras by the produce of their surplus eggs, which they carried to market in little osier hand-baskets.

Existence in such homes flowed smoothly, one year being exactly like another. The people had no prospects, no hopes, no ambitions. They lived from hand to mouth, and, while all went well, the produce of each day was sufficient for their simple wants.

Dr Wright wrote those words in 1893, when millions of people in England and Ireland lived more or less as the Brunty family lived. There are millions of people in the world today who live at that standard, or below, but in one respect Dr Wright was wrong. To say that the people had no prospects, no hopes, and no ambitions, is mightily to underestimate the human spirit. People will always have hopes and

ambitions; the Brunty family certainly had. With two small
sons in the family, and with expectations of more to follow,
they could not have been happy without hope or ambition.
And who can say that a simple life cannot be a happy one,
or that a simple diet cannot be a healthy one?

In 1898, Mr J. Horsfall-Turner, writing about the Brontë
family, went to Ireland to see the place where the father of
the Brontë sisters was born. In his book, *Bronteana*, he had
this to say about it.

The place was occupied by two goats when I saw it. A repulsive
feeling arises as you tread the mud floor, and it takes a strong
imagination to picture this birthplace of the Reverend Patrick
Brontë as a comfortable home even at the best.

It seems that Mr Horsfall-Turner was a victim of the material-
ism that was rising in the wake of the industrial revolution.
We have no reason at all to believe that the first home of
Patrick Brunty was anything but comfortable. It was certainly primitive, but no more so than most of the homes in
the area. In this home Hugh and Alice Brunty bore two
children who lived very long lives, and when the family
moved into another house nearby the only real difference
was that it was larger. As to the frugal diet, Hugh and Alice
had in all ten children, and nine of them lived into their
seventies; some of them, including the first two, lived to be
over eighty.

At this point we must look at the Brunty family in the
light of what was happening in the world about them. In
Ireland, between the beginning and the end of the eighteenth
century, the population grew from about one and a half million to about eight million; this in spite of extreme poverty
and wretched social conditions. The actual figures vary
because the practice of taking a ten-year census did not begin
until 1821; but all opinions agree that the population
explosion did occur, and for a variety of contributory

reasons. In her book, *The Great Hunger*, Cecil Woodham-Smith puts forward three main reasons for the rapid rise in population in Ireland. Firstly, there was an abundant supply of a cheap and easily produced food in the potato. Secondly, the miserably low standards encouraged early marriages. She quotes the Catholic Bishop of Raphoe as saying, 'They cannot be worse off than they are . . . and they may help each other.' Thirdly, there was no difficulty in finding somewhere to live, and although the home would be simple it would be warm. Of course it is never easy to explain why population explosions suddenly occur in any country. They happen, and the people living in the country are faced with many problems. The main problem in Ireland was that most people lived off the land, the supply of which cannot be increased. For this reason the land was divided into smaller and smaller pieces, many families trying to live on less than an acre. Against all this it must be said that the Irish love children and family life; and they are a people with a naturally cheerful disposition. Even so, all the factors were leading towards a disaster because the one thing that everyone depended on, the potato, was a very unreliable crop indeed. To quote Cecil Woodham-Smith . . .

There was too, barbarious and half-savage though conditions might be, one luxury enjoyed by the Irishman which favoured the survival and rearing of children – his cabin was usually well-warmed by a turf fire. Ill-clothed though he was, sleeping as he did on a mud floor, with his pig in the corner, the Irish peasant did not have to endure cold, nor did his children die of cold. They were warm, they were abundantly fed – as long as the potato did not fail.

Of course from time to time the potato crop did fail, but when Hugh and Alice Brunty were raising their family it did not fail in catastrophic proportions. That happened later, in 1845, by which time Hugh and Alice were in their graves, and their eldest son was the Reverend Patrick Brontë of Haworth in Yorkshire.

The ten children of Hugh and Alice Brunty came in quite a rare pattern: five boys followed by five girls. Patrick was born in 1777, and Alice, the last child, in 1794. Thus the marriage produced ten children in seventeen years. The record is as follows:

Patrick	1777	Jane	1789
William	1779	Mary	1791
Hugh	1781	Rose	1793 ⎫ twins
James	1783	Sarah	1793 ⎭
Welsh	1786	Alice	1794

The area where all the family were born and raised, and where all except Patrick lie buried, is only a few miles west of the mountains of Mourne. It is good farming land. Belfast is thirty miles to the north; Dublin is seventy miles to the south. In the years of Patrick's childhood, Belfast was a boom town, growing rapidly on the strength of the linen trade. Many thousands of Huguenot refugees from Catholic persecution had settled in the north of Ireland, and with them came the skills of spinning and weaving flax into linen cloth. As a young boy, Patrick Brunty was apprenticed into the trade and became a skilled weaver. Along with the prosperity which the linen trade was bringing to the north of Ireland there came a new political idea. Whereas previously the struggle had been between Protestant and Catholic, there came, at the end of the eighteenth century, the new and forceful idea that the two should unite in order to free the country from English rule. The Society of United Irishmen was founded in Belfast in 1791. Within a few years it led to an open rebellion, which failed and was ruthlessly put down by English troops. At the time of the rebellion Patrick, who took no part, was twenty-one years old, but his brother, William, fought in the rebellion and was lucky to escape with his life. Insurrections do not happen overnight. The ideas

which fuel them are discussed and debated in homes, and
wherever people meet outside. It is impossible to believe that
young Patrick Brunty did not talk about the politics of his
day. His father certainly did. Hugh Brunty never stopped
talking about the unjust laws by which the people of Ireland
were governed. And if we remember that Hugh was nomin-
ally a Protestant who had married a Catholic, it would be
natural for him to believe that the ideals of the United
Irishmen were similar to his own. Outside Ireland the period
between 1775 and 1800 saw two great revolutions carried to
their successful conclusions. The American colonists began
their struggle against King George's redcoats with what
looked like very slim chances of success, yet within a few
years they had won their freedom. The lesson did not go un-
heeded in Ireland. In 1789 the common people of France took
to arms against the government of aristocrats and land-
owners who ruled them. Again, victory seemed to come
easily. The opposing forces, which had looked so strong,
seemed to crumble away once the oppressed took to arms.
This gave strength to the feeling in Ireland that only when
people are prepared to fight for what they believe in can they
expect any change. In short, revolution was in the air. In
Patrick's home politics were as germane as their daily
bread. Their father spoke out loud and long against the evils
in Ireland. He blamed absentee landlords who had no interest in Ireland except for the extraction of rents; he spoke
against the Catholic and the Protestant churches for preaching hatred and distrust of the other; and against the King
and his government in England, who created and upheld laws
which worsened the lives of the common people in Ireland.
These were the ideas which Hugh Brunty was putting into
the minds of his sons, as vividly and as forcefully as he was
entertaining his friends and neighbours, who liked nothing
better than an evening by his fire. Hugh's eldest son, Patrick,
remained aloof from the political ideas which led to the
rebellion in 1798, unlike his younger brother. Patrick had

been bitten by another bug. In the Celtic spirit there is a reverence for learning, and in his home there were two books: the Bible, and a copy of *Pilgrim's Progress*. Patrick was taught to read and to write with the aid of these two books. As he grew older his passion for reading and learning became an obsession, and the theme of his study was constant. Only through God would the world ever change for the better, and that change must come from each individual. Patrick grew towards religion as a flower to the sun. He read everything he could lay his hands on but, of course, as he grew up there would be little reason for him to believe, or even to hope, that one day he would become a minister. That surely was quite impossible for the son of a man as poor as Hugh. Until he was sixteen or seventeen, Patrick's self-education was motivated solely from within; he wanted to improve himself. There was no particular end in view, and in these years it is extremely unlikely that anyone he ever knew or met could have dreamed where his desire for education was going to lead him.

In 1761, in Ballyroney, which is very close to the area in which the Brunty family lived, a son was born to a Presbyterian minister. The name of the boy was Samuel Neilson. In time he married the daughter of a wealthy merchant and became a merchant himself, in Belfast. Round about the year 1790 he became involved with politics, and in 1792 was appointed the editor of a new newspaper in Belfast. The *Northern Star* was totally involved with the ideas and beliefs of the United Irishmen movement, and was in fact the 'voice' of men like Wolfe Tone and Henry Joy McCracken. The first edition of the newspaper spelled out its aims on the front page:

To give a fair statement of all that passed in France, whither everyone turned their eyes; to inculcate the necessity of Union among Irishmen of all religious persuasions; to support the emancipation of the catholics; and finally, as the necessary, though not avowed, consequence of all this, to erect Ireland into a republic independent of England.

It is a statement of beliefs which all too clearly pointed ahead to the coming struggle. In 1798, when Patrick was twenty-one, and his brother William was nineteen, came the rebellion. Patrick kept well out of trouble, so did his father, but William took up arms with the United Irishmen. From the very beginning the insurgents were badly led and ill-disciplined. The English army had little difficulty in overcoming the rebels, and the United Irishmen never really stood a chance. William was at the battle of Ballynahinch, a town some fifteen miles south of Belfast, and a little less from where the Brunty family lived. The redcoats had occupied the town of Ballynahinch, which the rebels attacked at dawn on 13 June, but they were soon scattered, and pursued by cavalry units. Many of the rebels were killed in flight, but William Brunty managed to evade the soldiers. Later in the day he turned up at his home, where he hid. When the cavalry appeared at the door (as it happened they were Welshmen, regulars of the Welsh Horse), Hugh Brunty was able to convince them that nobody there had any interest in the battle of Ballynahinch. After the rebellion all the leaders were executed, as were many who had fled and were later arrested, so William was undoubtedly lucky to escape punishment for his involvement. The defeat of the United Irishmen was total and the movement collapsed. It seemed quite clear that whatever had happened in France and America was not going to happen in Ireland for a very long time.

A few years before the rebellion, John Wesley had preached an open sermon in a field near Rathfriland, half an hour's walk from the Brunty home. It is likely that Patrick was far more interested in John Wesley than the political figures of his day. John Wesley was leading a great crusade, and the power of his teachings was to affect Patrick throughout his life. Although he became an Anglican minister, the evangelical fervour of Methodism was very much to his liking, and eventually it was a Methodist organisation which took Patrick to Yorkshire.

Outside Ireland there were other young men who were beginning to make their way in the world. Horatio Nelson entered service in the navy in 1770. In 1779 Napoleon entered his military academy; and in 1787 young Arthur Wellesley, who was to become the Duke of Wellington, was given his first commission as Ensign with the 73rd Foot regiment. In time the careers of all these men would have a very strong effect on the life of Patrick Brunty.

And in 1779, the parsonage to the parish church in Haworth village, Yorkshire, was built. It was the same year that Hugh and Alice Brunty, with their two sons, Patrick and William, left the tiny cottage at Imdel with its two rooms, to move to a bigger house in nearby Lisnacreevy. It was only a mile, but the road to Haworth had begun.

As Patrick approached the age of fourteen his parents started looking around in the area for a job which might take the boy's interest. Patrick was most attracted to the trade of blacksmith; there was a forge in Ballynaskeagh where he often spent an hour watching the work in progress. He might well have become a blacksmith himself but the apprenticeship was for a set period of five years, and Patrick's father was against such a long period of training. Patrick's mother, Alice, had already taught her son a little about weaving, and it was natural enough that Patrick's parents should convince him of the bright future which the trade could offer. Their friend in Banbridge, Mr Robert Donald, who had a small weaving business, was doing well enough to be able to offer a two-year apprenticeship, and at the age of fourteen Patrick was taken on.

For two years Patrick worked hard to learn the trade and was soon making money. The revolution in France cut off the supply of linen to the English market, indirectly giving the trade to Ireland, and business boomed. When war broke out again with France, Patrick was given all the work he could cope with. When visiting Banbridge and Newry he could afford the luxury of buying books for himself. One book, Milton's *Paradise Lost*, so occupied his mind that he read it over and over again, and on one occasion it led to a punishment. Patrick had become skilled enough at weaving to operate his loom whilst at the same time reading a book propped against his machine. One day he was fined for imperfect work after one of his customers found fault with a finished cloth, and this troubled him, so he decided there would be no more reading whilst he was weaving. But his desire to read and learn was in no way diminished. Before leaving for work at the first light of day, and in the long evenings, Patrick read by the poor light in his home. In those days, artificial light in the home was provided by rushlight, a bunch of rushes dipped in tallow. Sometimes there were crude, home-made candles, and of course there was always the light from the fire. But all of these are poor lights, and to study by them is to risk damage to the eyes. In later life, Patrick's eyesight became very bad, no doubt affected by reading small print in a poor light as a young lad.

Chapter 6

The road to Cambridge

Patrick's obsession with *Paradise Lost* led to a chance meeting which changed his whole life. The man he met was a relative of James Harshaw, the gentleman farmer at Donough more who had once hired Hugh Brunty on Newry market, and for whom Hugh had worked when secretly courting Alice McClory. The Reverend Andrew Harshaw was a minister without a church. He had been trained as a Presbyterian, but although he was a highly educated and dedicated man, he lacked the one quality which in those days was a prime requirement for a minister, especially a Presbyterian; he had no pulpit personality. The faithful who attended Presbyterian churches demanded a minister who could hammer out the word of God without recourse to written notes, these people being more interested in how the sermon was put across than in its content, however learned and scholarly it may be. As Andrew Harshaw was not acceptable as a minister, he became the only teacher in a little school at Ballynafern, close to Ballynaskeagh, where he was in sole command.

Near to Imdel there is the relic of an old Irish fort, which had been an earthwork defence structure at the top of a slight hill. Today it is only a ring of trees crowning the hill, just as it was when Patrick Brunty used to go there. On a clear day, when he was not working, Patrick used to climb up to Imdel Fort and lie there reading. It is a very peaceful spot.

One Sunday afternoon, under a clear bue sky, with the mountains of Mourne to glance at when he lifted his eyes from his book, Patrick was reading his beloved *Paradise Lost*, and from time to time declaiming to the world at large. He was totally oblivious of the fact that he had an audience: the Reverend Harshaw, who was out walking. Having no gift for rhetoric, he was impressed by Patrick's rendition of the words of John Milton. He was certainly attracted to the lean, sandy-haired, young man who was thoroughly enjoying himself in this rather unusual way. In conversation, when the Reverend Harshaw learned that Patrick was a weaver with a burning desire to study, he offered to be his tutor, and at no cost to Patrick if he was prepared to study at times when both were free from other commitments. The offer was generous and seemed to Patrick to be an act of God, for from where else could he believe such good fortune to emanate? Andrew Harshaw had a good collection of books, and was a skilled and gifted teacher. The finest quality any teacher can have is the ability to recognise natural talent. Patrick Brunty was no ordinary weaving-lad; he was gifted, and what is equally important, he was prepared to work hard and long in order to realise his ambitions. At that time Patrick would not be able to define his ambitions, beyond expressing a vague desire to improve himself. All he knew was that he wanted to study, and that reading was his greatest pleasure. There was no end in view. It was enough that there were books to read, and things to learn, and a man had come along who was willing, and able, to help him.

After a year of study, done in the early mornings and late evenings when he was not weaving, Patrick was suddenly thrown out of work, when his employer at Banbridge died. But Patrick had money saved; he decided to cease working in the trade and to become a full-time student. There were no objections from his parents. They had taught him all they knew, and Hugh and Alice accepted that Patrick had left them far behind. The boy knew his own mind. Andrew Harshaw had told them that Patrick was a gifted scholar and had proved himself worthy of any chances that might come along. Within a few months that opportunity came. A teacher was required for the small Presbyterian school at Glascar Hill, near to Patrick's home, and the Reverend Andrew Harshaw was prepared to recommend his pupil. Further to this, the minister of Glascar Hill Presbyterian church was willing to recommend Patrick to the board of governors. As no other teacher was available, it looked certain that Patrick would be offered the position, but the board of governors rejected him. The reason given was that Patrick had a Catholic mother. He and his brothers and sisters had often been called 'papish bastards' by the village kids, which had meant very little to anyone, but now the slur had been taken up by men who should have known better. The board of governors defended themselves by pointing out the possibility that children of devout Orangemen might not be permitted to attend a school where Patrick Brunty was the teacher. The school existed by fund raising. The pupils paid a penny a week, plus a turf of peat every Monday morning towards the heating of the school. Other money came direct from the church. Most of the pupils were children of local farmers and work-people, many of whom were fervent Orangemen. The Bruntys were not a Catholic family, but their mother was born a Catholic and that was enough for prejudice to come into the picture. The news of the rejection must have hurt Patrick, but Hugh, who hated intolerance, would be furious. Alice had believed that the old prejudice towards her marriage had been overcome, but here it was, affecting the lives of their children. For a few days the family withdrew from friends and neighbours. It seemed that no-one could be trusted. But the Reverend Andrew Harshaw did not give up. He rallied the support of many Presbyterian ministers in the area who were willing to put their name to a second application for Patrick to be appointed. But by now, another candidate was applying for the post; a Presbyterian. At the last minute, however, he retracted his application, after a talk with Andrew Harshaw. In the meantime, the Reverend Alexander Moore, minister of Glascar Hill church, took it upon himself to appoint Patrick Brunty to the post. To the board of governors, the Reverend Moore asserted that he would take full responsibility. This was a brave move. The Presbyterian church is a very democratic organisation, and does not take kindly to clergymen acting without the express approval of the appointed elders and managers, so it is highly likely that the Reverend Moore would have suffered if Patrick Brunty had not been a success. As it happened, he was, and no child was withdrawn from the school. For Patrick, the change from weaver to teacher was the great turning-point of his life.

There can be no doubt at all that Patrick Brunty was a very good teacher indeed. He began without any formal training, but within a very short time his energy made the school at Glascar Hill a great success. His methods were quite simple; he believed in taking a personal interest in each of his pupils. There was but one class, and the age-range would be daunting, but Patrick set out to find the particular interest and capability of every one of his pupils. He went to talk to the parents of his charges. If a pupil was not bright, and the parents had little interest beyond getting the child out of the house for a while every day, Patrick advised them to keep the child at home, where there was much to learn that would interest the child. If a child was bright, and wanted to learn, Patrick went out of his way to ensure that the child was given every encouragement. He began evening classes too. He was a great believer in physical fitness; his classes always began with a series of gymnastic exercises and whenever the weather permitted he took his pupils out into the countryside.

Always a lover of nature, Patrick took care in introducing
to his children the beauty of the area in which they had been
born. On week-ends he sometimes took groups of the older
children to the mountains of Mourne. In winter he took
parties to the frozen lake at Loughorne. From some of these
countryside excursions the pupils returned with tales of the
high adventure that had befallen them, but most of this was
probably due to Patrick's sense of the dramatic. In the
1890s, when Dr William Wright was researching his book,
there were many tales of Patrick and a group of boys being
lost in a thick mist in the Mourne Mountains and another
tale of a party making their way across a frozen lake
with the ice cracking beneath their feet. The adventures
had turned into legends. The hero was, of course, the
young teacher who brought his party of children through
all the danger to their homes. But all these tales illustrate
the fact that Patrick loved nature, and believed quite
simply that God can be seen as well in the great outdoors
as in a church. It is also clear that Patrick was a popular
man.

At this time in his life, when Patrick was not yet twenty,
he started to write poetry. Later in his life, after he had
been to Cambridge University, Patrick had a volume of his
poetry published at his own expense, but much of it
had been written when he was the schoolmaster at Glascar
Hill.

It cannot be said that Patrick's poetry has any great
merit; but it is passionate, and it is revealing. He was
desperately trying to express himself in poetry as he had seen
his father express himself by the spoken word. One of his
poems tells us a lot about the mind of Patrick Brunty as
a young man. He did not include it in his volume, which was
published after he had become a minister of religion, and it
is not difficult to see why. The young Patrick had no reason
to be cautious. In this poem he really lets himself go; it is
a poetic imitation of his father at his best.

Vision of Hell

At midnight, alone, in the lonely dell,
Through a rent I beheld the court of hell;
I stood struck dumb by the horrid spell
Of the tide of wailing that rose and fell.

The devil sat squat on a fine-winged throne;
Before him in ranks lay his victims prone;
In anguish they praised him with sullen groan,
Like an ocean that never ceased to moan.

At a signal they sprang from their burning bed,
And through the sulphurous flames, by devils led,
In many dances they onward sped,
As they followed the devils who danced ahead.

'Enough!' yelled the fiend from the fine-winged throne,
'Of posture-praise from my subjects prone,
Of torture, shrieks, and of sullen moan,
Of many dances and stifled groan.

'Each to his post in my burnished state.
Ye clergy, who fed the fires of hate,
Neglected the poor, and cringed to the great,
Ye shall roast in honour within my grate.

'I dread no foe but the Christ of God;
Through you, His clergy, I feared his rod;
But you took his pay and obeyed my nod,
And you drove the poor from their native sod.

'Ye landlords can only have second place,
In devilish deeds ye were first in the race;
But no treason to Christ mixed with your disgrace,
Ye were mine from the first, and in every place.

'Attorneys and agents, I love you well,
But you throng with your numbers the courts of hell;
Bastard-bearers and bailiffs need place as well,
For their hellish deeds no tongue can tell.'

The cottage in Ballynaskeagh, where Alice McClory lived as a girl
BELOW The church at Magherally where Hugh Brunty and Alice
McClory, parents of Patrick Brontë, were married in 1776

The tiny cottage at Imdel where Patrick Brontë was born on St Patrick's Day in 1777

BELOW The church at Drumballyroney where Patrick and his brother William were christened and where many of the Brunty family are buried

The first page of the Register of Baptisms at Drumballyroney Church. A cross on the right of the page marks the entry for William, Patrick Brontë's brother. (The church register containing the entry for Patrick's baptism has been lost.)

A view from the glen showing the house near Lisnacreevy where Hugh and Alice Brunty brought up their family of ten children. The McClory cottage is next to it.

BELOW The school at Glascar Hill where Patrick was first employed as a teacher

Patrick Brontë as a
young man

The title pages of
Patrick Brontë's works

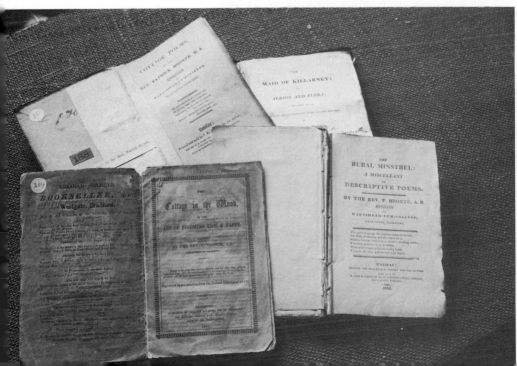

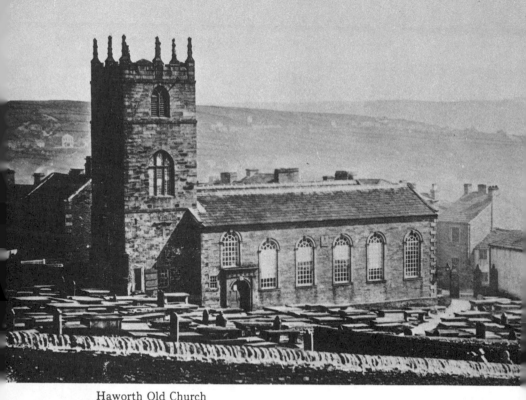

Haworth Old Church

BELOW Haworth Main Street

Haworth Old Rectory, where Patrick Brontë raised his four surviving children

LEFT Branwell Brontë
RIGHT The Brontë sisters: *left to right* Anne, Emily and Charlotte

Rev. Patrick Brontë *c.* 1856

The unveiling in 1956 of the plaque commemorating the birthplace of Patrick Brontë. The two girls are Emily and Anne Brontë, direct descendants of Patrick's brother William.

The clergy aloft on a burning floor
Sat slaking their thirst with bastard's gore,
And gnawing the bones of the murdered poor,
The evicted who died on the silent moor.

The landlords were penned in a fiery fold
And drank from a furnace of molten gold
The rent they had wrung from their tenants of old,
Who had laboured and died in hunger and cold.

And the men who had paid for love by lust,
And were false in return for confiding trust,
In a slimy pit they were downward thrust,
Through a scum that was foul with a fetid crust.

And a cry arose like the thunder's roar
As the devil stood forth on the burning floor,
And the fiends with a shout stood up to adore,
And the earth-rent closed and I saw no more.

The poem, and others like it, was often used in the school
as an exercise for copying and for reading aloud. Much of
this particular poem is a reflection of the opinions of
Patrick's father. There is a great deal of Hugh Brunty's
philosophy in what is being put over. In the verse beginning,
'The clergy aloft on a burning floor', there is a direct
reference to one of Hugh's tales about the vestry tax on
foundlings for conveyance to the foundling home. Here again
is the old story of how Welsh came to be adopted into the
Brunty family; and of the way that some people took the
money supposedly for carrying the infants to the home but,
instead, murdered them and pocketed the cash. The tax was
still in force when Patrick was teaching at Glascar Hill
school. Clearly, Patrick blamed the clergy for supporting the
law; and the landlords and the law also come in for their
share of criticism. At the age of twenty, Patrick already had
some very definite ideas about what was wrong in the Ireland
of his time.

When some of Patrick's brighter pupils reached the age

at which they would normally leave school, he took it upon himself to plead with their parents for them to be allowed to stay a little while longer to complete their education. Many children stayed on an extra year, whilst others began work but continued to attend the evening classes. It was this, and Patrick's great burst of poetic energy, that led to a disaster. The school was a success, and so was Patrick, but he fell a victim to his own passion.

The relationship between pupil and teacher is fraught with many dangers, not the least of which is the intimacy which can create many problems for the unwary. A girl, the daughter of a farmer, had been allowed to stay on at the school after an appeal by Patrick to her parents. She had red hair, and no doubt at the age of fifteen or so she was very attractive. She fell head over heels in love with her teacher. Evidently Patrick allowed the romance to develop, and on one occasion one of the girl's brothers saw Patrick kissing his pupil behind a haystack, and told his parents. The circumstances were more than enough to turn a very minor affair into a major scandal. When they confronted their daughter they found her totally unrepentant and very angry indeed at their interference in her love affair. Further to this, her parents found poems that Patrick had been writing to the girl, the content of which could only mean one thing: the relationship between the two was not merely that of teacher and pupil! In any rural area this sort of incident can shake every household, and in Ballynaskeagh the story was blown up out of all proportion. Unfortunately for Patrick, the father of the girl was one of the managers of the school. Equally unfortunate for Patrick, a new minister had just been appointed to the church, and the man who had known Patrick for so long was no longer in the area. The school was immediately closed down, throwing Patrick out of a job, and for a reason that looked like ending his career as a teacher. Patrick was by no means sorry for what he had done, and he let everyone know that he had little respect for their morality. He declared that he was in love with the girl, and that everyone would have to accept that fact (shades of his father) because true love was pure, and would prevail in the end. Patrick spent the best part of a year working in the fields, trying to convince himself that he still loved the girl, but he and his red-haired Juliet (unlike Hugh Brunty and Alice McClory) drifted apart. She found someone else, and married him, whilst Patrick went on writing his poetry. He must have believed that his teaching career had come to a swift and final end.

At the time of the 1798 rebellion Patrick was unemployed. No doubt he was too occupied with his personal problems to get himself physically involved with the United Irishmen as his brother did. In the wake of the abortive rebellion came the manhunts, the summary trials and executions, and the common sight of the military roaming the land. The war between England and France was continuing; there was common talk that the French were preparing an invasion fleet intending to put a large army on English soil, but the navy stood in the way of the all-conquering Napoleon, and the name of a great hero was on everyone's lips. Admiral Nelson had won a great victory against Egypt in the Mediterranean Sea, and was raised to the peerage, with the given title of Baron Nelson of the Nile. Handsome gifts were presented to him by Turkey and Russia; the King of Naples conferred on him the title of Duke of Brontë, with an estate in Sicily valued at £3,000 per year, and in the city of Naples, Admiral Nelson met for the first time the wife of the English Ambassador, Sir William Hamilton.

In Ireland, the almost penniless Patrick Brunty, working now as an agricultural labourer, was interviewed by Reverend Thomas Tighe, Rector of the parish of Drum ballyroney, for the post of school teacher. The Reverend Andrew Harshaw – Patrick never had a truer friend – had spoken to the Reverend Tighe, giving an account of Patrick's full record at the school in Glascar Hill, including the unfortunate love affair. To his eternal credit, the Reverend Tighe set aside this petty scandal. He wanted a good teacher not only for the school but also for his own children. He took to Patrick immediately, and offered him the post, which was gratefully accepted. Thomas Tighe was a rich man, a friend of John Wesley, who had stayed in his home when preaching at Rathfriland a few years before. Patrick Brunty must have thought it the greatest piece of good fortune he ever had when he was made schoolteacher at Drumballyroney. But there was much more to come from the meeting with the Reverend Thomas Tighe. The Rector was also a graduate of St John's College at Cambridge.

From the very moment when Patrick began to teach at the school in Drumballyroney, his feet were set firmly on the road which would take him away from Ireland. He was a teacher again, older and wiser. The mistake he had made at Glascar Hill was not likely to be repeated. At Drumballyroney he was being paid more money than he had hitherto earned, and in addition there was extra money to be earned from private tuition. These lessons were given by Patrick in the grand house, employing liveried servants, where the Reverend Thomas Tighe lived. He was a respected and learned gentleman. His voice carried a lot of weight not only in the church but in society in general. No-one quarreled with his opinion of the new schoolmaster, so Patrick was in a position of some strength. It is probable that, had he so wished, he could have spent his life in the profession, and to good effect, for he had all the necessary qualities and he enjoyed the work. However, within a short time of meeting the Reverend Tighe, Patrick was being persuaded that his true calling was the church. He became a regular attender at the church services in Drumballyroney, and some of his brothers and sisters were brought along too. It was through Patrick's association with the church and school there that, for the first time, the Brunty family became church attenders. The association with Drumballyroney has continued to the present day and many of the family are buried there.

The Reverend Tighe gave Patrick the idea that it was possible, if he continued his studies under the Reverend Andrew Harshaw, and saved money, for him to contemplate applying to the Reverend Tighe's old college, St John's at Cambridge, for admission as a sizar. The college prided itself on its policy of admitting a few highly rated scholars who had little money, but it was by no means an easy road. The places were few and there were always many applications for them from England, let alone Ireland. And even if Patrick were granted a place, he would have to support himself financially for four years. The Reverend Tighe was able to advise Patrick on the various small financial awards that were available on exhibition of merit. These chances were there but, again, they were very seriously contested and could certainly not be counted on. The basic finance would have to come from Patrick himself.

As the new century was dawning Patrick reached the age of twenty-three. He was doing well at his job and saving money. His friend, Andrew Harshaw, continued teaching Patrick, and gave him the confidence to look beyond the area in which he had been born; beyond Ireland itself, to England and a university education. It was a very great challenge. Patrick was a bright and hard-working student, but to consider leaving a safe job, with a good future, in order to attend at St John's, and to maintain himself there for four years, took a lot of courage. It took a lot of faith too, from the people who were behind Patrick and believed he deserved the chance. As for his mother and father, what could they have thought about it all? It was a world about which they knew nothing. The five girls ranged from eleven down to six years old. All their sons were now earning money, working for employers, and the family were better off than they had ever been. Only Patrick had shown any interest in education, and he was old enough to know his own mind. If he wanted to go to England, then it was best for him to do so. All the same, in their hearts, they must have wished that he would be happy to stay in Ireland, teaching at Drumballyroney.

But it was not to be. The applications to St John's College were accepted. In 1802 Patrick had confirmation that a place in the college had been reserved for him. Came the day when, in September, he put together a few personal possessions and his precious books, and set off from Ballynaskeagh to Warrenpoint. The ship that was to take him to England lay in the harbour, and Patrick remembered perhaps his father's tale of the little orphan stowaway who became the first Welsh in the Brunty family. Soon he was aboard the ship, watching the mountains of Mourne slip away from him.

A surprise awaited him when he arrived at Cambridge after the long journey. There was a letter from Ireland addressed to himself at St John's College. Inside the letter was a gift of five pounds. Patrick never disclosed from whom that gift came. All he ever said about it was that it came from an old friend in Ireland. The money was no doubt very welcome, as he had little money when he arrived at Cambridge, but the thought that lay behind the letter and the gift must have meant even more. Patrick was alone in England, but he was not without friends.

Patrick's arrival and enrolment at St John's must have raised a few elegant eyebrows. The college prided itself on its policy of having a liberal attitude towards the backgrounds from whence some of its students came; nevertheless it is doubtful if the college had ever had a student from as poor a background as Patrick Brunty, who arrived wearing the homespun clothes made by his mother. He was also considerably older than most of the new entrants: a tall, lean Irishman with a shock of red hair, practically penniless, innocent of the world outside of rural Ireland, and terribly

anxious to work. This last impression would cause most of
the wry smiles. It was an age when young men went to great
pains to appear indolent and sophisticated. At the beginning
of the nineteenth century, most of the young men at Cambridge were sons of the landed gentry who ruled the country.
Their future was secured, regardless of whether they studied
well or badly at university. Their fathers' wealth and reputation had put them in the college, and should the young
rascals misbehave, the same wealth and reputation would
find a place for them in decent society. In their world, the
sight of a poor, and zealous, Irishman constituted no threat
whatsoever, and could only be highly amusing.

Entrants to the university were divided into three classes
of society. At the top were the fellows, who were fee-paying
and totally supported by their families. The second class
were the pensioners, who were paying reduced fees, and had
some academic attainment behind them. At the bottom of
the order were the sizars, the sons of poor men who could
not afford to maintain their children at university, however
bright they were.

Patrick got off to a good start. In the Register of Residence
his name went down on 3 October 1802, and before Christmas
he had won his first exhibition. It was the Robson Exhibition, a cash award on which Patrick could draw until com-
pleting his studies. It was no great amount, but every little
bit was going to count, and now Patrick knew that the advice
given to him by the Reverend Tighe was wise. He was going
to be able to survive. Incidentally, the name written in that
Register of Residence is Patrick Branty. At some point later,
the surname Branty has been partly erased, and the name
Bronte substituted.

In the following year, 1803, Patrick won two more awards
from exhibitions. The Sir Ralph Hare exhibition was for
'thirty of the poorest and best-disposed scholars'. The money
for this charitable award came from the rent of the Cherry
Marsham estate in Norfolk. The Duchess of Suffolk award

was also Patrick's throughout the four years of his attendance at Cambridge. Yet, even with these three exhibitions to his credit and support, Patrick was finding it hard to exist. He was by no means a profligate man; most of the time he lived on porridge oats, and his clothes were patched and darned by himself; but he needed money for books and for his lodgings.

He had made some new friends at St John's. John Nunn was five years younger than Patrick, from a middle-class background; their friendship was to continue for many years after they both became curates in the Church of England. Another friend was able to help Patrick with some money. Henry Martyn was a Cornishman, who had entered the college in 1797 at the age of sixteen, and in 1802 was made a Fellow of St John's. He had some influential friends in the Church Missionary Society, and was, in fact, destined to become a missionary himself. In February 1804, Henry Martyn wrote a letter to William Wilberforce, an old-boy of St John's and a force in the administration of the Church Missionary Society Fund. The letter pleads the case of Patrick Brontë – by this time Patrick was writing his surname in this way – and goes on to say that Patrick could manage to live comfortably with a grant of twenty pounds a year. The letter adds, cautiously, that Patrick might be able to manage on less. William Wilberforce wrote an endorsement on the letter. 'Martyn about Mr Brontë. Henry Thornton and I to allow him £10 each annually.'

It is possible that at this time Patrick was thinking of becoming a missionary. He had come under the influence of Charles Simeon, the curate at Trinity Church, Cambridge, who was a founder member of the Church Missionary Society, under whose auspices Henry Martyn left Cambridge in 1805 to become a missionary. It is likely that Patrick intended to follow him.

The same year, Nelson won his great victory and died at Trafalgar. The name of Brontë now assumed an aura of hero-

ism. Napoleon was massing a fleet of barges in Boulogne with
the intention of invading England. To this day, the Martello
towers stand along the coasts of England and Ireland as a
reminder of the fears of that time. At Cambridge, Patrick
joined the Corps of Volunteers, who drilled with wooden
staves, training to resist the invading French forces. One of
the young men training with Patrick was John Henry
Temple, an aristocrat from the Irish branch of the family,
and destined to become the great Tory statesman Lord Palmerston. Patrick left Cambridge a convinced Tory, a political persuasion which was to last throughout his life. He also
became a hero worshipper of Nelson, and later of the Duke
of Wellington.

Patrick had no sympathy for the Irish who plotted rebellion against England. Whilst Patrick was at Cambridge yet
another insurrection in Ireland failed disastrously; this one
led by Robert Emmet who was later hanged in Dublin. In
any case, Ireland and England were now joined legally under
the Act of Union 1802, and it seemed clear to Patrick that
the future of all his countrymen, and certainly his own
future, lay in the direction of solidarity with the English
cause. Ireland was a poor country, divided against itself, and
suffering greatly for its continued antagonism towards England. A sensible man, emerging from an education at one of
England's oldest and most respected universities, would
have been unlikely to think in terms of going back to Ireland
to make his future there.

In his final year at St John's, Patrick won another exhibition award, and in April 1806, he took his degree as Bachelor
of Arts. In August of that year he was ordained by the Bishop
of London in the Bishop's Palace. There was a minor hitch,
due to the fact that Patrick had no birth certificate, but a
declaration from the Reverend Tighe as to where and when
Patrick had been born was accepted, and Patrick was duly
licensed as a curate in the Church of England. He was
appointed curate to the parish church at Wethersfield in

Essex. The metamorphosis was complete. At twenty-nine years of age the Irish boy with a love for books had become the Reverend Patrick Brontë. In December 1807 Patrick was ordained an Anglican priest by the Bishop of Salisbury. His stipend at Wethersfield was sixty pounds a year. Patrick had achieved his first ambition but another ambition was burning inside him. He was going to become an author. He was determined that the name Patrick Brontë was going into the annals of English literature.

Chapter 7

The Reverend and Mrs Brontë

During his time at Cambridge Patrick was strongly influenced
by Charles Simeon, an evangelical preacher who, in 1782, had
been appointed a life-long fellow of King's College, and was
the perpetual curate of Trinity Church. He was in his forties
when Patrick first listened to his powerful sermons. Charles
Simeon had been a prime mover in the formation of the
Church Missionary Society in 1799. Henry Martyn was one
of his dedicated followers, and it was through Patrick's
association with these two men at Cambridge that he came
to the notice of the Reverend Joseph Jowett, the Regius Pro-
fessor of Civil Law at Cambridge. He was also the vicar of
Wethersfield, a small village only about fifteen miles from
Cambridge. Joseph Jowett was an evangelist, and when he
sought a curate for his church at Wethersfield it was natural
for his choice to fall on Patrick Brontë. The young Irishman
had done well at Cambridge. He was a devout Christian, a
friend of Henry Martyn, and could become a candidate for
a Mission later in his career. No doubt these factors were
borne in mind when the Reverend Jowett appointed Patrick
as his curate.

But within a very short time of his arrival at Wethersfield
Patrick had to face a serious emotional crisis. He fell in love,
proposed, and was accepted; and later walked away from
the agreement. None of this was done lightly. Throughout

his life Patrick Brontë was a serious, strong-minded man, not easily dissuaded from his beliefs. At the age of thirty, newly appointed to Wethersfield, Patrick met a young parishioner and made up his mind that she would become the wife he wanted. The objection to the proposed marriage came from the girl's family, but in the end it was Patrick who retracted his proposal. The love affair took place between the autumn of 1806, when Patrick arrived at Wethersfield, and the autumn of 1808, by which time he had made up his mind to leave the area. He left Wethersfield in 1809 and never returned there.

Patrick's first duty as a curate in Wethersfield was in August 1806. His name first appears in the Register of Baptisms, certifying that he was the officiating minister. Early in 1807 Patrick met Mary Burder. She was eighteen and the elder of two sisters. There was one brother. Their widowed mother, who was quite wealthy, lived in a large farmhouse at Finchingfield Park, near Wethersfield. Evidently Patrick was struck by the innocent beauty of the young Mary Burder; and the fact that she would bring with her an income of some kind no doubt helped in his choice. The friendship was approved for a time, until the Burder family realised what Patrick's intentions were. In December 1807 Patrick went to London for the ceremony of ordination as an Anglican priest; and it is possible that soon after his return to Wethersfield he took the opportunity to propose marriage. Never one to dally once he had made up his mind, Patrick acted quickly, and the Burder family were taken by surprise. Their strong reaction was equally surprising to Patrick. Mary had accepted him – there is no doubt of that – but the family did not and they made it very clear. They saw Patrick as an upstart Irishman with no money behind him. They had other ideas for their Mary. She was a pretty girl, and there was enough money in the family to attract a husband with more than a poor curate could offer. Mary Burder's brother had a furious row with Patrick. Harsh words were spoken, and from that moment Patrick's relationship with Mary was totally opposed by her family. Many years later, when Charlotte Brontë told her father that she wanted to marry *his* curate, who happened also to be an impecunious Irishman, Patrick objected just as strongly as Mary Burder's brother had done.

Throughout the year 1808, Mary Burder was kept under family care and protection. Having been told that he was unacceptable to the family, Patrick went through a deal of soul-searching, and finally gave up his courtship. In November 1808, writing to a friend, Patrick explained his feelings about the love affair:

Since I returned here, I have enjoyed more peace and contentment than I expected I should have done. The lady I mentioned is always in exile; her guardians can scarcely believe me that I have given up the affair forever.

Patrick had also decided to put some distance between himself and Mary Burder. The friend he had met at St John's, John Nunn, had found a position as curate in Shrewsbury. From there he wrote to Patrick, telling him about a vacancy that existed in nearby Wellington. Patrick's abortive love affair was enough reason to decide on a move. In a letter we can divine the soul-searching which led to his decision:

All along I violated my conscience and my judgement. 'Be not unequally yoked', says the Apostle. But Virgil was not far wrong when he said, 'Omnia vincit Amor', and no one can deny Solomon's authority, who tells us that 'Love is stronger than Death'. But for Christ's sake we are to cut off a right hand, or to pluck out a right eye, if requisite. May He by His grace enable me always to conform to His will.

Patrick had been doing some reading and a lot of hard thinking, probably assisted by some counsel from his vicar, the Reverend Joseph Jowett, who happened to be a Yorkshireman and given to plain speaking. In January 1809 Patrick officiated at a funeral in Wethersfield, but soon afterwards he appeared in Wellington, where he found himself joint-curate with a certain William Morgan, who was to become a life-long friend. Wisely, Patrick put the affair with Mary Burder behind him and threw all his energies into his new job.

During the time he was at Wethersfield Patrick had paid a visit to his old home in Ireland. Not much is known about the sentimental journey; in fact many writers believe that after leaving Ireland to go to Cambridge, Patrick never went back to see his family. But this would have been very improbable. Although he certainly kept distant from his family, there is no reason to believe that he cut himself off entirely. It is on record that he occasionally sent small gifts of money home to his mother as long as she lived. There is also clear evidence that he kept up a correspondence with his family. The letters were rare, but they were never unfriendly. Patrick's youngest sister, Alice, gave a statement about the family to the Reverend J. B. Lusk, who visited her shortly before she died at the age of ninety-seven. Obviously she was of an age when her memory might not be relied upon; but about her brother Patrick coming home she had no doubts at all: 'Patrick came home after he was ordained, and preached in Ballyroney. All our friends and neighbours were there, and the church was very full.' The church was the one which Patrick had attended, next to the school where he had taught. In the year 1897 one of the church wardens was a William Brontie (a most unusual way of spelling the surname), a great-grandson of Patrick's brother William. It seems that the whole family in Ireland became quite closely connected with the church in Drumballyroney.

The journey home to Ireland, and the holiday spent amongst his family and friends, must have been very memorable for Patrick. One cannot help wishing that he had put his feelings down on paper, but if he did, nothing has ever been found. Perhaps one day something more reliable than his sister's statement may come to light. His parents were growing old; his father died in 1808, the year after Patrick's visit. All his brothers were now over twenty-one, and doing very well for themselves. William was married, but he lived near to his old home. The eldest sister was eighteen; the youngest, Alice, was thirteen. Now that Patrick was a minister of the Church of England he knew that his own future lay away from the family, and this would bear on his mind. The tales that tell of this last visit home all mention that Patrick spent a lot of his time roaming alone in the countryside, deep in thought. Perhaps his relationship with Mary Burder was on his mind also.

Fifty years or so later, in 1857, a niece of his old friend from Cambridge, John Nunn, was staying with her uncle at Thorndon, in Suffolk, where he was the rector. Patrick was still alive, but all his children were dead, and he was alone at Haworth. John Nunn's niece recalled that one day her uncle appeared with a large batch of letters in his hand. He told her that the letters had been written to him by Patrick Brontë, and that they referred to his 'spiritual state' at one stage of his life. John Nunn then made a very tantalising statement to his niece: 'I have read them once more, and now I destroy them. He was once my greatest friend.'

The lady was not permitted to look at the letters before they were destroyed. What Patrick had written in those letters will, now, never be known. But there is reason to believe that all of them were written at a time when Patrick was under great stress, after leaving Cambridge, and before leaving Wethersfield. John Nunn chose to destroy them, and in doing so considered he was protecting Patrick's interests. Since the death of Charlotte Brontë, interest in the whole family was growing rapidly, and the letters might have caused Patrick some pain. At the time, John Nunn's decision was wise and loving, but we must, today, deeply regret that they were not placed into safe keeping for a few more years.

The year 1809 was a fateful one for Patrick Brontë. Early in January he arrived in Wellington, Shropshire, to take up his new post as joint-curate in the parish church there. Patrick had put Wethersfield and Mary Burder behind him: 'Oh! that I could make my God and Saviour my home, my Father, my all!' Those words are contained in a letter to a friend, written from Wellington. Such a state of religious fervour is often the result of being thwarted in love. Patrick was now determined to throw himself into the service of God, and at Wellington he met a man with similar passions. Apart from the fact that they were both curates, the two men shared another interest. Both of them longed to express themselves by means of the written word. William Morgan, a Welshman, was already writing religious articles and tracts to good effect. His views were the same as Patrick's; the word of God must be taken into the homes of the people, and social progress could only come from a basis of Christian principle. At the time there was, throughout the land, a great religious revival, which was being spearheaded by the Methodists and the evangelists. Both Patrick Brontë and William Morgan were curates in the established church but in terms of their religious expression they were among the many who were crying out for change. They both believed, wholeheartedly, that the word of God had to be taken to the people; and that then, and only then, would the people come to the church. They formed a deep friendship at Wellington, which was to last throughout their lives.

Through his association with William Morgan, Patrick first began to feel that his own desire to write could be part of his service to God, and not something he did for himself. William Morgan believed that all talent was God-given, and that to use a talent in the service of God was to complete the cycle. The power of the written word, be it prose or poetry, has lasting value. It could be an extension of the pulpit sermon; it could go into the homes of the people and be read there by more than one pair of eyes. On this basis, Patrick began to think about putting together a collection of his own poems, encouraged by William, who could see the religious foundations in the thoughts. William knew how to get his own work printed. Now, together, they would become authors. Their whole relationship was centred on this idea.

Before the end of 1809 both men had left Wellington and moved to separate curacies in Yorkshire. No-one can be certain what it was that attracted them to that county. William Morgan did know some prominent Methodists there, and that could have led to the moves; but perhaps it was more the very nature of Yorkshire itself that was the incentive. Yorkshire was one of the most prominent centres of the revivalism that was sweeping the country. It was a tough, wild area, far removed from the gentle civility of the south. To be a successful preacher in Yorkshire called for a forceful spirit and a hardy body. The people there were dour and uncompromising, but they took their religion seriously.

By the end of 1809, William Morgan was curate at Bierley, near Bradford, and Patrick Brontë was curate at Dewsbury. Their parishes were only five miles apart. Both areas were the same, filled with the dark, satanic mills of the industrial revolution. Patrick's first duty at Dewsbury was to officiate at the wedding of one John Senior to a Miss Ellen Popplewell. Neither could write their name in the marriage register, so they signed with a cross and a thumb-print. Patrick signed his own name with a flourish.

The vicar of the parish church at Dewsbury was the Reverend John Buckworth, an outspoken preacher, and a confirmed evangelist. He had written some hymns, and religious tracts, which had been published in Dewsbury by a printer who was a personal friend. The relationship between John Buckworth and his new curate was very friendly.

Patrick lived in the vicarage with the family, having his own study, where he often dined alone, but otherwise he was treated as one of the family. The vicar often teased Patrick about his Spartan eating habits: Patrick had a liking for simple oatmeal porridge, a relic from his home life in Ireland and the lean years at Cambridge. But on Sundays, Patrick always joined the family at their table.

In the church, Patrick was not considered to be as good a preacher as John Buckworth, partly because of his pronounced Irish accent, which some of the Yorkshire people found very difficult to understand. However, he spent much of his time visiting parishioners in their homes – the sick, the elderly, and so on – and within a few months he became totally accepted. Yorkshire folk do not take readily to strangers, but Patrick had a lot of charm, and he was very sincere in everything he said and did. It was enough to win them over to him, in spite of his accent.

At this stage of his life Patrick Brontë was a very different fellow from the sad, old man whom the world found at Haworth after Charlotte had died. At Dewsbury Patrick was enthusiastic, hopeful, overtly friendly, and filled with the joy of a religion in which he utterly believed. He spent much time in the Sunday school, teaching the young children, where his great flair for teaching earned him respect and admiration.

At Whitsun, in 1810, something happened which rightly earned for Patrick the respect of the whole congregation of his church. The story is very Irish in character – the Man of God who is not averse to using his fists in a righteous cause – and Patrick was fond of telling the story.

In the north of England, at Whitsuntide, it is a very old custom for the churches and Sunday schools to combine together to form a procession through the town. The various groups march behind banners, often led by a band, from their churches and chapels to a rendezvous in the centre of town, there to hold an open-air combined service. After this the procession moves on to some prearranged site in the countryside where a programme of sports and competitions is played out, and food and drink is taken. The 'Whitsun Walks', as they are called, are a joyous part of the religious calendar. In the year 1810, Patrick was walking with his congregation through the streets of Dewsbury when a group of bullies made a nuisance of themselves. One of the men, a well-known local with a reputation for drinking and fighting, held up the column of marching children on a narrow bridge. There was some confusion until the Reverend Patrick became aware of what was happening, whereupon he swiftly pushed aside the trouble-maker, and the column continued towards the countryside for their afternoon of sports and games. The bully went about the town declaring that he would 'get' the curate when the procession was on its way back to town. This threat swept through the pubs of the town, where the non-religious were conducting their own Whitsun celebrations. The result was that a large crowd was waiting by the narrow bridge when the procession returned. The local tough was now very much the worse for drink, and was shouting that he would soon put the Irishman in his place. As the column of marchers approached the bridge the bully pushed through the waiting crowd and confronted Patrick. The crowd waited for the next move that would undoubtedly begin the fight they were all anticipating. They saw Patrick take up a firm stance between the bully and the children, clearly ready to fight. It soon became obvious however that the bully had suffered a change of heart, because when Patrick took a step towards him the bully retreated, and a wave from Patrick set the procession moving again. The crowd howled with laughter as the bully tried to explain that he had meant the whole thing as a joke. The confrontation was over without a blow being struck. From that moment on, Patrick was a greatly respected man in Dewsbury.

Shortly after this event a young boy was rescued from drowning in the river Calder, which flows through the town.

The boy, who was somewhat retarded, had fallen in the river when playing with some other boys. Almost certainly he would have drowned but for the chance that Patrick was out on one of his country walks. He jumped in the river, brought out the boy, and carried him to his home. There Patrick refused all help, and left for the vicarage. Of course, the news was all over Dewsbury in a short time.

One other incident occurred for which Patrick is remembered in Dewsbury. For some reason the vicar, John Buckworth, was away from his church, and Patrick had been left in charge. The bellringers wanted to practise for a coming competition, but they had neglected to get the permission of the vicar. When Patrick heard the bells ringing he went to the church, and demanded to know what was going on. When he heard that they had not asked for permission he ordered them out of the church. The leader of the bellringers tried to argue but Patrick raised the shillelagh he was carring. The men left forthwith! There was some bad feeling afterwards, and the chief bellringer resigned, but the vicar supported Patrick. By this time all Dewsbury had come to accept and respect their Irish curate.

In the novel *Shirley*, by Charlotte Brontë, there is a clergyman who acts fearlessly when confronted by danger. The incident on the bridge at Dewsbury is almost identical with a situation in Charlotte's novel. Perhaps it is yet another example of the fact that when Patrick told a story it was remembered not only factually but emotionally, as if the hearer had personal knowledge of the events.

Aside from all this Patrick was earnestly developing the power of his pen. He was often seen to be writing in a note-book, in the garden of the vicarage, and during his country walks. Probably with the aid of his vicar, Patrick found someone willing to publish his work. He prepared a volume of his poetry and paid the cost of printing. This became the slim volume with the title of *Cottage Poems*, a copy of which exists today in the Brontë Museum at Haworth. In his own words, Patrick describes the book as being written for 'the lower classes of society', which might today be considered an offensive phrase, but Patrick intended it merely to denote those people who had to work for their daily bread. *Cottage Poems* contains a wide choice of Patrick's work; many poems were written when he was teaching in Ireland, some of them are from his days at Cambridge, and some are from the time he was at Dewsbury. The whole work is of slight literary value, but as an insight into the mind of the young Patrick Brontë it is invaluable. At the beginning of the book is what is called 'the advertisement', which is merely the introduction, and is written by Patrick himself although he refers to himself in the third person:

When relieved from clerical avocations he was occupied in writing the 'Cottage Poems' from morning till noon, and from noon till night, his employment was full of indescribable pleasure, such as he would wish to taste as long as life lasts. His hours glided pleasantly and almost imperceptibly by, and when night drew on, and he retired to rest, ere his eyes closed in sleep with sweet calmness and serenity of mind, he often reflected that, though the delicate palate of criticism might be disgusted, the business of the day in the prosecution of his humble task was well-pleasing in the sight of God, and by His blessing might be rendered useful to some poor soul who cared little about critical niceties.

Those words were read by all Patrick's children. The book of poems, and others written by their father, were on the shelf in the parsonage at Haworth, and were often used as aids in schooling the children. They grew up in the knowledge that their father was a poet, an author, a literary man, and a churchman. It was quite obvious to them that the greatest pleasure of all was to be found in creative writing.

One last tale from Dewsbury needs to be told. Patrick often wrote letters to the local papers; on one celebrated occasion becoming involved in a fight for justice on behalf of a poor

young man, who had been imprisoned for the offence of
desertion from the army. His family produced evidence that
their son had been wrongly convicted, but without the means
of going to the law on the matter, they went to see the Irish
curate. Patrick took up the case, and began a campaign including writing letters to William Wilberforce and the Minister
of War, who at the time was none other than Patrick's associ-
ate at Cambridge, John Henry Temple, now the Tory politi-
cian Lord Palmerston. Lord Palmerston intervened, and the
imprisoned man was released. The whole episode stands very
much to Patrick's credit, and no doubt his children were told
the tale many years later. Their father was never afraid
to fight for what he believed in, and if that meant putting
up his fists – well – that too, if there was no other way of
gaining justice.

Whilst Patrick was at Dewsbury, his friend William Morgan, at Bierley, was making the acquaintance of a young
lady, Jane Fennel, the only daughter of John Fennel, a
Wesleyan preacher. Through William Morgan, Patrick met
the Fennel family, and became a frequent visitor to their
home. The Fennels had relations living in Cornwall, one of
whom was a young lady called Maria Branwell, whom
Patrick was soon to meet.

Although Patrick stayed for only eighteen months at
Dewsbury the short time was of great importance. In the
year 1810 Patrick celebrated his thirty-third birthday; eight
years had passed since he left Ireland, and his chosen career
as an Anglican minister was developing well. There had been a
somewhat shaky beginning, because of the abortive love affair
with Mary Burder, but the move to Wellington, and from
there to Dewsbury, had put Patrick on an even keel once
more. He was doing what he really wanted to do; and doing
it with success. The Reverend John Buckworth certainly
appreciated the efforts of his Irish curate, and the town of
Dewsbury accepted Patrick with a growing fondness.
Patrick liked the town, and he liked the people of Dewsbury.

He was finding something in the hardy, rough and ready spirit of Yorkshire with which he could identify. After all he had spent his first twenty-five years in Ireland, and his character was well formed before he left there. True, he had spent four years at Cambridge in the company of men from wealthy backgrounds, but he had not changed much. He still chose to live, eat, and dress simply. The people who lived in Yorkshire were not alien to Patrick. They lived in a hard climate; had to work hard for their living; and were thrifty, and God-fearing. The great majority of them were from what Patrick had termed 'the lower classes of society', similar to Patrick's own background. His nine brothers and sisters in Ireland were still living in a similar environment. Patrick was the only one of the family who had received an education and had raised his social status, but fundamentally he had not changed. He was a simple man who saw his future as an educator and minister to simple people. *Cottage Poems* was addressed to them. The working classes of Yorkshire were Patrick Brontë's chosen people. For this reason, more than any other, he remained with them to the end of his life.

In March 1811 the Reverend John Buckworth offered Patrick an opportunity for promotion. The church of St Peter's at Hartshead, which lies a few miles west of Dewsbury, required a minister, and John Buckworth had the responsibility of making the appointment. He offered it to Patrick and he readily accepted. At Hartshead he would be his own master; at the same time he would be able to call upon John Buckworth for help and advice. The two men had become firm friends, and continued to be so long after Patrick left Dewsbury. At Hartshead Patrick found lodgings at Thorn Bush farm, which was the home of the Bedford family, because the church of St Peter's had no place of residence for the incumbent. The origins of the church go back to the fourteenth century, and when Patrick Brontë began his ministry there he found a thriving congregation. The previous minister had founded a Sunday school, which Patrick was delighted to take on. His stipend, on appointment, was sixty-two pounds per annum, which was more than enough for his simple wants at the time. In the church registers we can see that the churchwardens wrote his name as either Bronty or Brunty, but Patrick's own signature is very clearly P. Brontë, after which he adds the word 'Minister'. It was the first time he had been empowered to do so.

These were good times for Patrick. As the minister to his own church, continuing his attempts at authorship, and also for the first time in his life being free from financial stress, he was enjoying life. From this time he began to send money home to his mother in Ireland in generous amounts, and he also began the practice of an annual collection in his church for 'the poor in Ireland'. He was a popular figure in local society, attending many social functions and private house-parties. A portrait of him, painted at this time, shows him as a handsome man, wearing side-whiskers but without a beard. It is the face of a proud man, with humour, and his eyes are compelling. Like most Irishmen he was an amusing conversationalist, and was never afraid to speak his mind. He regularly contributed articles and letters to the *Leeds Mercury* and the *Leeds Intelligencer*, which added to his status as a literary man, concerned with what was going on not only in his area, but in the world in general. Politically he was an ardent Tory. Soon after he arrived in Hartshead, Patrick's conservative beliefs brought him into danger. Characteristically, Patrick spoke out strongly against law-breaking, and adopted the habit of always carrying with him a loaded revolver.

In Yorkshire, a great deal of unrest was being caused by the introduction of machines into the textile industry; unemployment was increasing, the Luddite Riots were spreading. The riots took their name from a certain Ned Ludd, a man of low intelligence, who had wrecked machinery in the stocking industry in Nottingham, and his followers were committed to a programme of violence. The Reverend Patrick

Brontë took a hard line against the rioters, and became unpopular with his congregation for it. His attitude has been
misunderstood; he was never against the working class as
such, but he was opposed to anyone who broke the law of
the land.

About this time there occurred a very violent attack on
a mill near to Hartshead, in which two men were killed and
several wounded. The mill-owner had soldiers assisting him
to defend the mill, and therefore the workers' attack constituted an armed rebellion against the state, for which seventeen men were later condemned to death. The riots were very
serious, and for his outspoken criticism, Patrick Brontë was
at risk. No attack was ever made on him, but he went about
his duties with the revolver in his coat pocket. Perhaps it
was because this fact was well known, and because he had
a reputation for fearlessness, that nothing more than threats
ever came his way. He obviously told his children about
these events and Charlotte was so impressed that she chose
the Luddite revolts as a background to her novel *Shirley*.
In Hartshead, Patrick is remembered for his openly stated
opposition to the Luddite gangs; but he is also said to have
arranged for secret burials in the churchyard. Men who were
killed in the rioting, or mortally wounded, were quietly and
unofficially buried at night. The story goes that although
Patrick condemned the riots he had mercy for those who
were killed, and for their families. The story of the attack
on Rawfolds Mill is told by Mrs Gaskell in her *Life of
Charlotte Brontë*:

> Mr Cartwright was the owner of a factory called Rawfolds, in
> Liversedge, not beyond the distance of a walk from Roe Head.
> He had dared to employ machinery for the dressing of woollen cloth,
> which was an unpopular measure in 1812, when many other circum-
> stances conspired to make the condition of the mill-hands unbear-
> able from the pressure of starvation and misery. Mr Cartwright
> was a very remarkable man, having, as I have been told, some
> foreign blood in him, the traces of which were very apparent in

his tall figure, dark eyes and complexion, and singular, though
gentlemanly bearing. At any rate, he had been much abroad, and
spoke French well, of itself a suspicious circumstance to the
bigoted nationality of those days. Altogether he was an unpopular
man, even before he took the last step of employing shears, instead
of hands, to dress his wool. He was quite aware of his unpopularity,
and of the probable consequences. He had his mill prepared for
an assault. He took up his lodgings in it; and the doors were
strongly barricaded at night. On every step of the stairs there was
placed a roller, spiked with barbed points all round, so as to impede
the ascent of the rioters, if they succeeded in forcing the doors.
On the night of Saturday the 11th of April, 1812, the assault was
made. Some hundreds of starving cloth-dressers assembled in the
very field near Kirklees that sloped down from the house which
Miss Wooler afterwards inhabited, and were armed by their leaders
with pistols, hatchets, and bludgeons, many of which had been
extorted by the nightly bands that prowled about the county, from
such inhabitants of lonely houses as had provided themselves with
these means of self-defence. The silent sullen multitude marched
in the dead of that spring night to Rawfolds, and giving tongue
with a great shout, roused Mr Cartwright up to the knowledge that
the long-expected attack was come. He was within walls, it is true;
but against the fury of hundreds he had only four of his own
workmen and five soldiers to assist him. These ten men, however,
managed to keep up such a vigorous and well-directed fire of mus-
ketry that they defeated all the desperate attempts of the multitude outside to break down the doors, and force a way into the
mill; and, after a conflict of twenty minutes, during which two
of the assailants were killed and several wounded, they withdrew
in confusion, leaving Mr Cartwright master of the field, but so dizzy
and exhausted, now the peril was past, that he forgot the nature
of his defences, and injured his leg rather seriously by one of the
spiked rollers, in attempting to go up his own staircase. His dwelling
was near the factory. Some of the rioters vowed that, if he did
not give in, they would leave this, and go to his house, and murder
his wife and children. This was a terrible threat, for he had been
obliged to leave his family with only one or two soldiers to defend
the house. Mrs Cartwright knew what they had threatened; and
on that dreadful night hearing, as she thought, steps approaching,

she snatched up her two infant children, and put them in a basket up the great chimney, common in old-fashioned Yorkshire houses. One of the two children who had been thus stowed away, used to point out with pride, after she had grown up to woman's estate, the marks of musket shot, and the traces of gunpowder on the walls of her father's mill. He was the first that had offered any resistance to the progress of the 'Luddites' who had become by this time so numerous as almost to assume the character of an insurrectionary army. Mr Cartwright's conduct was so much admired by the neighbouring mill-owners that they entered into a subscription for his benefit, which amounted in the end to £3000.

Mrs Gaskell wrote her vivid account of the attack on the mill some forty-five years after the night on which it happened. It must have been the main topic of conversation for miles around. The whole of the area was seething with discontent at the time, and it is not surprising that Patrick, whose church was only two miles away, took to carrying a loaded pistol with him wherever he went.

A new school, a Wesleyan academy, had been built at Woodhouse Grove, near Bierley, where William Morgan was the incumbent. John Fennel had been appointed Governor and Headmaster of the academy, and William Morgan was courting his daughter. In the year 1812, Jane Fennel became twenty-one. She had written to her cousin Maria Branwell in Cornwall, inviting her to stay with the family for a while. Maria, who was twenty-nine and unmarried, had lost both her parents only a few years before. She had been born on 15 April 1783 into a middle-class family living in Penzance. Her father was a merchant. There was one son, and Maria was the third of four daughters. When her father died in 1808 he left in his will an annuity of fifty pounds to Maria. By a coincidence, Maria's father died in the same year as Patrick's father. For a description of Maria we can do no better than read what Mrs Gaskell said of her.

Miss Branwell was extremely small in person; not pretty, but very elegant, and always dressed with a quiet simplicity of taste, which accorded well with her general character, and of which some of the details call to mind the style of dress preferred by her daughter for her favourite heroines.

Maria arrived in Yorkshire in the summer of 1812, and within a few days she met the thirty-five-year-old Patrick Brontë in the home of her cousin Jane. Mrs Gaskell describes him as follows:

> Mr Bronte was the incumbent of Hartshead; and had the reputation in the neighbourhood of being a very handsome fellow, full of Irish enthusiasm, and with something of an Irishman's capability of falling easily in love.

From the very first meeting, Patrick was captivated by the shy, small, well-mannered Maria. For her part, Maria was overwhelmed to find how quickly she fell in love. Very soon, in a letter to Patrick, written from the home of her uncle, Maria says,

> ... when I consider how short a time I have had the pleasure of knowing you, I start at my own rashness, my heart fails, and did I not think that you would be disappointed and grieved at it, I believe I should be ready to spare myself the task of writing.

The couple saw a lot of each other in that summer of 1812, when William Morgan and Jane Fennel became engaged to be married. The foursome made many visits to the countryside, and before the end of August Patrick had decided that Maria was for him. His friends the Fennels and William Morgan all agreed that the match would be a good one. John Fennel appointed Patrick to be school examiner at the Wesleyan academy; his duties began in August. And so from a financial point of view Patrick saw no need of a lengthy courtship. Maria was free to make up her own mind. The annuity which she had inherited was not a great one, but it would provide a healthy addition to Patrick's stipend. Taking all these circumstances into consideration, Patrick proposed an early marriage, and Maria accepted him. In a letter she makes her feelings plain:

...but I cannot allow that your affection is more deeply rooted than mine. However, we will dispute no more about this, but rather embrace every opportunity to prove its sincerity and strength by acting, in every respect, as friends and fellow-pilgrims travelling the same road, actuated by the same motives and having in view the same end.

Maria Branwell was a gentle lady, and more conditioned by the mores of society than Patrick ever was. But in letters written to her lover at the time of his whirlwind courtship of her, it is plain to see that Maria was not by any means a timid woman.

Oh! what a sacred pleasure there is in the idea of spending an eternity together in perfect and uninterrupted bliss.

Unless my love for you were great how could I so contentedly give up my home and all my friends – a home I have loved so much that I have often thought nothing could bribe me to renounce it for any great length of time together, and friends with whom I have been so long accustomed to share all the vicissitudes of joy and sorrow? Yet these have lost their weight, and though I cannot always think of them without a sigh, yet the anticipation of sharing with you all the pleasure, and pains, the cares and anxieties of life, of contributing to your comfort and becoming the companion of your pilgrimage, is more delightful to me than any other prospect which this world can possibly present.

I love you above all the world.

I am certain no one ever loved you with an affection more pure, constant, tender, and ardent than that which I now feel.

When I work, if I wish to get forward I may be glad that you are at a distance.

I firmly believe the Almighty has set us apart for each other;
may we, by earnest, frequent prayer and every possible exertion,
endeavour to fulfill His Will in all things.

Love letters are the concern of only two people, and these
letters from Maria to Patrick would never have been read
by anyone else but for the fact that long after Maria was
dead, Patrick gave his daughter Charlotte a packet of letters which he suggested she should read. Writing about this,
Charlotte said, 'The papers were yellow with time, all having
been written before I was born. It was strange now to peruse,
for the first time, the records of a mind whence my own had
sprung ... I wish she had lived and that I had known her.'

Sadly, Maria Branwell did not live long enough for any
of her children to know her. But for her love letters, which,
thankfully, Patrick kept, the world would have known very
little about the mother of the Brontë sisters. She has often
been portrayed as a pious, meek, and refined woman. This
may well have been her public face, but in her private relationship with Patrick we can see that she was no less passionate than he was, and as outspoken. Had she lived, it is likely
that her character would have had a great influence on her
children, at least equal to that of their father's. But in that
event it is also very likely that her daughters might not have
written their novels. The genius of the Brontës was forged in
the tragedy of their home-lives.

In the 1813 edition of the *Gentleman's Magazine* a notice
appeared:

Lately, at Guisely, near Bradford, by the Rev. W. Morgan,
Minister of Bierley, Revd. P. Brontë, BA, Minister of Hartshead-
cum-Clifton, to Maria, third daugther of the late T. Branwell, Esq.,
of Penzance. At the same time, by the Rev. P. Brontë, Revd. W.
Morgan, to the only daughter of Mr John Fennel, headmaster of
the Wesleyan academy, near Bradford.

The double wedding was celebrated on the 29th December 1812. Each man, now a fully fledged minister, officiated at the other's wedding. On the same day, in Penzance, Maria's younger sister, Charlotte, was also married. It was the end of a fateful year. Patrick Brontë and his wife Maria, deeply in love, settled into a house at Hightown, near Liversedge, where the Luddite attack had taken place.

Chapter 8

The Bruntys in Ireland

When Patrick Brontë was at Hartshead, there occurred an
event in Ireland which Patrick must have read about. It was,
in effect, a microcosm of the struggle for dominance between
the Catholics and the Protestants who were living there. It
concerned a fight between one of Patrick's brothers and a
Catholic neighbour by the name of Sam Clarke. In itself it
was no more than a fist-fight between two men in a field,
watched by a few thousand people from the area. But the
scrap was so memorable that it was remembered in great
detail by people who actually saw it, and by others who were
later told the tale. At the end of the century, almost ninety
years later, the story of the fight was known to many people
living in County Down; and when William Wright was
researching for his book, *The Brontës in Ireland*, there were
plenty of people who were able to tell him about the fight
between Welsh Brunty and Sam Clarke.

It took place in the year 1811, in a field owned by a farmer,
Mr John Barr of Ballynafern. Patrick's youngest brother,
Welsh, who was twenty-five at the time, was courting a girl
by the name of Elizabeth Campbell, whom he later married.
Her younger brother, who was attending school, was a delicate boy, slightly deformed, and he walked with the aid of
crutches. Some of the older boys were given to tormenting
the little cripple at times, by no means a rare thing in any

part of the world. When on one occcasion he arrived home daubed with mud, his sister Elizabeth told her fiancé about it. Welsh decided to stop the tormenting once and for all, and went to see the father of two of the older boys who were ringleaders of the gang.

Sam Clarke was about thirty years old, and had the reputation of being handy with his fists. Welsh asked Sam Clarke to put a stop to the tormenting of the crippled boy; and at some point in the conversation, Welsh said that if nothing was done, he, Welsh, would put a stop to it himself. Angry words were used by both men, and when Welsh was told to mind his own business the conversation ended. The next day, Welsh took up a position from where he could see the children coming across the fields from the school at Ballynafern. He saw the crippled boy being attacked; the older boys had taken his crutches, and had dumped him in a pond with the water up to his neck. The children were dancing around the pond chanting 'clashbeg, clashbeg', which means 'telltale'. Welsh grabbed the two Clarke boys before they realised what was happening and forced them into the water. Then he made them carry the crippled boy home.

That night, Sam Clarke challenged Welsh Brunty to a fight. The challenge was accepted, and the news spread like a bush-fire through the villages of Ballynaskeagh, Imdel, Lisnacreevy, and far beyond. A professional pugilist, living in Newry, was brought in to make the necessary arrangements. Seconds were appointed, and a suitable site was found for the battle. The men would fight in a dip in a field circled with a protective cordon of rope. Beyond that would be a ring of men calling themselves 'special order preservers'. The crowd could place themselves on the rising ground around the hollow. The time was fixed for noon on a chosen day.

Meanwhile, both combatants began to prepare themselves. By the appointed day the reason for the fight had been forgotten in the general excitement. All that mattered was that there was to be a fist-fight between two men; and that was a lot more exciting than a cock-fight, which was one of the standard entertainments of the times. Sam Clarke was Catholic, and Welsh Brunty was Protestant, which added spice to the proceedings. And as a wise man once remarked, if there's anything the Irish like better than a fight, it's two.

The day dawned warm and dry. Long before noon a great crowd had assembled in the field at Ballynafern. It was said that Sam Clarke's mother had told her son he would not be welcome in her house again if he did not 'lick the mongrel'. The word was often used to describe the Bruntys. They had a Catholic mother! Probably because most of the crowd who had come to watch the fight were Protestants, Welsh enjoyed popular support, but Sam Clarke was older, and bigger, and he had declared that he was going to beat the hell out of Welsh Brunty. The contestants approached the ring. Sam Clarke was accompanied by his wife, and Welsh had Elizabeth Campbell, his sweetheart, by his side. With the professional pugilist acting as referee, the men stripped to the waist, and after a quick word with the two men the referee stepped back and the battle was on. It lasted at least three hours on that warm afternoon. There were no rules, but it appears that both men made it a fair fight. In the early stages Sam Clarke had the advantage but as the day wore on Welsh was tiring far less than his opponent. At a critical moment, Elizabeth Campbell's voice rang out loud and clear from Welsh's corner. 'Welsh, my boy! Go in and avenge my brother, and the mongrel!' Her exhortation was to be recalled for many years. It encouraged Welsh, who tore into battle with such fervour that the last few minutes caused some of the spectators to faint. Sam Clarke finally went down to a furious barrage of blows. As he could not rise, the fight was over, but Welsh would accept no congratulations until Sam Clarke had been carried away to his bed.

There were two interesting results from the fight. From that day until they were both old men, the two were close friends and often together. Also, the fight became a point in time against which lesser events were measured. Such-and-such a child was born two years after the fight between Welsh Brunty and Sam Clarke. So-and-so married so-and-so the year before the fight. For this reason many people knew about the fight but not the reason for it. The last word on the fight must rest with a certain Reverend W. J. McCracken, who wrote to William Wright as follows:

I can bear my personal testimony to the gratifying fact that Welsh Brunty lived to regret the fight. The only time I ever heard him refer to it was one day in my father's house. An old man chanced to come in who hadn't seen Welsh for a long time. He approached with a great 'How-do-ye-do?' adding, 'Och, Welsh, God be wi' the times when you licked Sam Clarke'. The old flatterer evidently thought that Welsh would be hugely pleased; but the only answer he gave him was in these words: 'All folly, all folly, all folly, but folk won't see their folly in time.'

The words of Welsh Brunty are as true today as they were then.

At the time of the Welsh Brunty–Sam Clarke battle, the Brunty family in Ballynaskeagh were doing very well for themselves. Close to the cottage where their father had first met Alice McClory, they had built a larger two-storeyed house, which is still standing, and indeed is lived in today. (The smaller McClory cottage is now used as a store but is in good condition, and negotiations are in progress to preserve it.) William Brunty, the second eldest son, had married. He lived very near to the rest of the family, as did Red Paddy McClory, their uncle. William, Hugh, and Welsh Brunty worked on road construction. The land on which they lived belonged to the Sharman family, who were model landlords, intent on improving their estate. The other Brunty brother, James, was a shoemaker. The closeness between the family was very understandable. After all, they were the result of a marriage between a Catholic and a non-

Catholic, and this fact alone set them apart from their neighbours. The eldest son had gone to Cambridge university and had become a clergyman. No-one from Ballynaskeagh had ever done that before; and when I paid a visit there in 1979 it was pointed out to me that no-one had ever done it since!

But there were other factors which set the Brunty family apart. Physically they were all tall. Hugh Brunty was known as 'Giant Hugh' so he must have been well over six feet. And all the Brunty daughters were tall girls, well above the height of the average man at the time. This may partly account for the fact that only one of them married. The four sons and five daughters all contributed to the family income and shared duties. They farmed the land surrounding the glen close by, and there were enough of them to provide the tight social group which gave them the reputation of being aloof. Two of the sons played the fiddle, and the girls were often seen dancing with their brothers in the glen. It is easy to see that any young man taking a fancy to one of the Brunty daughters faced a fairly daunting prospect. The Bruntys were different folk; they kept themselves to themselves. No wonder they were known as a 'dangerous and outlandish family'.

Another reason why the family were held in awe by their neighbours was that they lived immediately by a glen which had a long reputation of being haunted. Not only did they live near the glen, but their amusements were held there, and so closely were the family linked with the glen that it became known by the locals as the Brunty or Brontë glen, as it is today. The history of the glen and the history of the family became so entwined that some of the locals believed the family were in league with the devil. Every year, on the eve of May, the family went into the glen, dancing and picnicking through the last day of April, and afterwards they hung garlands of wild flowers gathered from the glen inside and outside their houses. Long before the first day of May became associated with Labour and Communist movements, it was a most important day in the calendar of the 'old religion' which we know as witchcraft. Small wonder that the Brunty family had quite a reputation in County Down, long before Patrick's children became known to the world.

Four ghost-stories were connected with the glen before the Brunty family lived there. Legend has it that a young man murdered his sweetheart there. That night as he lay in his bed he was visited by her ghost, which called to him through his window. The man cried out and, reaching to embrace the spirit, fell out of the open window and was found dead outside his house. The story goes that the two separate spirits are now seen, always crying out, endlessly searching for each other.

Another story concerns a robbery. A stream runs through the glen. At a certain point where an easy crossing could be made, a man was set upon by two thieves who cut his throat. When the dying man was found later, he could still manage to talk, but only in a whisper. The gash in his throat was oozing blood. The men who found him said that by putting an ear close to the dying man's lips they could hear him say, 'Ten pennies in my pocket.' It was all he said before he died. When Patrick's father, Hugh Brunty, used to tell this story he had a way of whispering the words, 'Ten pennies in my pocket', which made the flesh creep. Of course, it is said that on certain nights in the glen the whispered words can still be heard.

One of the ghosts of the Brontë glen has no known story to explain why she is there. She is an old woman, carrying a child wrapped in a shawl. If you happen to meet the woman she will ask you for a night's lodging, but she averts her face from you as she does. Then, whatever your reaction to her, she exposes her face, a grinning skull. The spirit then disappears, laughing.

The ghost of the headless horseman is, perhaps, the best known of all the tales told about the glen. This particular story is connected with Giant Hugh, Patrick's brother. Before the Bruntys came to live near the glen there were stories of a ghostly horse passing through thickets where no horse could pass, ridden by a figure dressed in flowing robes. The man's boots were firmly in the stirrups, his hands held the bridle; but where his head should have been there was only a red and jagged stump. The man is thought to be someone who left the area to go to fight as a soldier. In some foreign land he charged into the attack, and the slash of a sword removed his head. Now, and perhaps forever, he is trying to find his old home.

Giant Hugh Brunty comes into the story because it is said that he and a friend were once in the glen when the headless horseman was seen. Hugh's friend stood rooted to the spot, but Hugh went towards the spectre without any fear. Just as Hugh reached the apparition, his friend saw it disappear. Hugh Brunty returned laughing and would say nothing to anyone about what he had seen or done. But this was common to all the Brunty family; when folk talked about ghosts and unearthly happenings, the Bruntys smiled. And if their smiles were thought to be enigmatic, well, the Bruntys said that people could believe whatever they wished.

When the potato blight hit the area, causing such misery, Hugh carried a basket of rotten potatoes to the glen. He was seen there, calling out to the devil, and throwing rotten potatoes into the glen. Ever since, an area in the glen is known as 'The Devil's Dining Room'.

Only one Brunty daughter, Sarah, married. At one time she went to live next door to a house where a man named Frazer had committed suicide. When Frazer's ghost began to bother Sarah and her husband, Simon Collins, she talked to her brother Hugh. Although he was eighty-two years old at the time, he decided to rid her of the ghost. For several nights he went to the house where Frazer had died. First he took a gun with him, but the ghost did not appear. On the following night Giant Hugh took his fiddle with him, and was heard playing it in the empty house, but again the ghost did not appear. When he returned home, Hugh was delirious and took to his bed in great pain. He said that a huge frog with claws was on his chest, trying to crush him. Before he died he swore that he would make sure that Frazer's ghost would never appear again. He died that night in 1863, in the house which stands today, overlooking the glen, and the ghost has never appeared since.

Hugh was buried beside the little schoolroom in the grounds of Drumballyroney Church, where most of his brothers and sisters lie buried. A headstone was recently placed on the mound, commemorating the family.

Chapter 9

The end of the road

The Reverend Patrick Brontë and his wife, Maria, had their
first child at Hartshead, near Bradford, in Yorkshire, late
in the year 1813. The actual date of the birth is not known,
but the christening was held on 23 April 1814. William
Morgan was a godfather; Jane Morgan and her mother, Mrs
John Fennel, were godmothers. The child, Maria, was named
after her mother. The baptismal register reads: 'Maria,
daughter of Rev. P. Brontë, minister of this church, and
Maria his wife.' It was the very first time that a mother's name
was included in the register at Hartshead. Obviously this was
an innovation of Patrick's, in honour of his wife.

In the same year as the birth of his first child, Patrick had
his second volume of verse published. He entitled this one
The Rural Minstrel, and in it was a poem he had written to
his new wife. In the poem are the lines:

> Maria, let us walk, and breathe the morning air,
> And hear the cuckoo sing,
> And every tuneful bird, that woos the gentle spring.

On the second anniversary of her wedding, Mrs Maria Brontë
was heavy with her second child, Elizabeth, who was born
in February 1815. Maria's sister Elizabeth Branwell came
up from Cornwall to help with the confinement, so no doubt
the child was named in her honour.

After two years of marriage, and four years at Hartshead, Patrick now received an offer to move on. The minister of the Anglican church at Thornton was anxious to move to Hartshead, because he was courting a Miss Walker who lived at Lascelles Hall. Miss Walker was wealthy, and her fiancé wanted to live as close to her as he could. He proposed an exchange of duties with Patrick Brontë. The reason given for the exchange was one which would be fully understandable to Patrick, but the ministry at Thornton was worth a good deal more in straight financial terms; and this no doubt attracted Patrick with his young family. At about the same time, their friends John Fennel and William Morgan were also involved in changes. John Fennel left his post as headmaster of the Wesleyan academy, to become curate to the Bishop of Bradford, John Crosse; William Morgan became minister of the new Christ Church in Bradford. This would have influenced Patrick's decision. The exchange was agreed upon. Patrick and Maria, and their two small children, Maria and Elizabeth, moved to Thornton in May 1815.

The three families were now living in roughly the same area. William Morgan was publishing in Bradford a magazine called *The Pastoral Visitor*. Patrick Brontë contributed to it, and in 1815 William Morgan wrote in his magazine a review of Patrick's latest literary effort. This time it was not a collection of poems, but a prose tale entitled, 'The Cottage in the Wood'. Patrick introduced his tale with these words:

An account of a pious family, consisting of an aged couple and a virtuous child, whose appearance and education qualify her for a higher position in the world than that of a cottager's daughter. Accident brings to the door a young man in a state of almost helpless drunkenness ...

The tale was too short to be called a novel but it was a departure from Patrick's usual writings. His friend William Morgan reviewed it as follows:

This is a very amusing and instructive tale, written in a pure and plain style. Parents will learn in this little book the advantages of Sunday schools, while their children will have an example well worthy of close imitation. Young women may here especially obtain a knowledge that the path of virtue leads to happiness. We would therefore most cordially recommend this book to all sorts of readers.

Patrick had paid for the cost of printing, as he did with all his work; and this volume, like its predecessors, did not sell enough to defray his expenses.

By the end of 1815 Maria was expecting her third child, and Aunt Elizabeth Branwell was still staying with the Brontës, helping her sister to run the home and look after the two young children. On 21 April 1816, the third child was born. This time the Brontës named their child after another Branwell sister, Charlotte.

The Battle of Waterloo had ended the Napoleonic wars, and Europe was now at peace. Patrick Brontë greatly admired the Duke of Wellington who was Commander-in-Chief of the victorious Allied Powers. This is hardly remarkable, for the Iron Duke was one of the greatest figures of the times, but in later times Charlotte Brontë held the Duke in high esteem and this must have been a direct influence from her father.

In July 1816 Aunt Elizabeth went home to Cornwall, and the Brontë family took on a servant girl called Nancy Garrs. By the end of the year, Maria Brontë was expecting her fourth child. She had been married for four and a half years when her son, Patrick Branwell, was born on 26 June 1817. The frequent pregnancies were beginning to affect her health, but there is plenty of evidence to show that, at Thornton, the Brontës led a happy life, with many friends, and Patrick was a kind and considerate husband.

Thirteen months after the birth of Patrick Branwell, the fourth daughter came into the world. Emily Jane Brontë was

born on 30 July 1818. It was now necessary for a second servant to be taken on, so Nancy Garrs brought her younger
sister, Sarah, to help with the rapidly growing family. Very
soon Maria Brontë was again pregnant. The sixth child was
to be her last. Anne Brontë was born on 17 January 1820.
The family of husband and wife, six children and two servants, were crowded into the small house in Market Street,
Thornton, which still stands today. It was the birthplace of
the three Brontës who achieved fame; and it was the place
where Patrick Brontë spent his happiest years. There, he
wrote his last imaginative work, which he called 'The Maid
of Killarney'. After the family left Thornton, Patrick gave
up trying to achieve literary success. But a copy of each of
his four published works stood on the shelves in his home
for his children to see as they grew up.

It was ambition that took the Reverend Patrick Brontë from
Thornton to Haworth; and the tragedy of his life began
there. From the time of his arrival in Haworth his happiness
was doomed, because to a very large extent it centred upon
his family life, and when the family got to their new home
Maria Brontë was already ill with the cancer that would
cause her death. From that moment on, Patrick was never
the same man.

In a letter written to a friend, a few years after leaving
Thornton, he said, 'I have never been very well since I left
Thornton. My happiest days were spent there.' In another
letter, written when he was an old man, he recalls the happy
days before sadness descended upon his life: '... and I can
fancy, almost, that we are still at Thornton, good
neighbours, and happy with our wives and children.'

The first idea of the move came in May 1819 when the
Reverend J. Charnock, incumbent at Haworth since 1791,
died. At nearby Thornton, Patrick would be one of the first
to know. The curate at Haworth was advised to carry on
until a successor was appointed. Haworth had a very special

reputation in religious circles. From 1742 to 1763 the incumbent was the Reverend William Grimshaw, an important figure in the evangelical movement of the eighteenth century, who was known as 'the Apostle of the North'. There were other reasons why Patrick Brontë was attracted to the parish. The living there was a perpetual curacy: that is, once appointed, the incumbent retained it for life, and no-one could take it from him. The parsonage which went with the curacy was on the same terms. The salary of the minister, which accrued from fixed rents, was higher than the salary afforded by Thornton, and was very secure. There is a possibility that Patrick also thought Haworth might be a healthier place to live than Thornton, but this is doubtful because the village had a bad reputation for health, and Patrick lived near enough to be aware of that fact. However, it is on high moorland, and maybe Patrick liked what he saw when he walked over there.

Under an ancient law, dating back to Elizabethan times, the curacy at Haworth could only be granted with the full approval of the trustees, added to that of the Bishop of Bradford. For some reason the Bishop of Bradford neglected to speak to the trustees before making his appointment, and there began a trial of strength between the Bishop and the trustees. For a few months Patrick was unsure what would be the outcome. He was appointed to the position; he walked over there several times and met the trustees; but the struggle for power continued and eventually Patrick tendered his resignation without having taken up his duties. Then the Bishop of Bradford appointed the man who had been acting curate, the Reverend Samuel Redhead. The trustees were furious. The people of Haworth reacted strongly, and violently, and after three mad Sundays the Reverend Redhead fled the village. The position was again open. Patrick Brontë was again offered the curacy, this time with the approval of the trustees added to that of the Bishop of Bradford, and in February 1820, the licence was given

by the Archbishop of York. The long battle was over.
The dour and watchful people of Haworth had made their
point. In Patrick Brontë's licence there appears a clause
which spells out the trustees' rights in every future appointment. The clause was a tacit surrender by the Bishop of
Bradford.

In April 1820 Patrick and his family loaded their possessions into the seven horse-drawn carts. Some of the horses
had been sent over from Haworth by one of the trustees.
They represented a mark of respect for their new man,
Patrick Brontë. Throughout the struggle with the Bishop of
Bradford, the trustees had learned something of Patrick's
courage and wisdom. At one point they had suggested
that Patrick should serve a trial period before being
appointed, but his reply made it abundantly clear that he
would do nothing of the kind! The villagers of Haworth
were impressed. Patrick Brontë was a man to be reckoned
with.

Patrick, Maria, their six small children, and the two servants finally moved into the parsonage, which overlooks the
bleak graveyard. It was bleaker in 1820 than it is today, lack-
ing as it did any of the trees that now soften the view.
Through the spring and summer they settled into the parsonage, which was to be the last home for Patrick and his
family. The children went for long walks on the moors which
surround Haworth. Their mother was often confined to her
bed, and in January of the following year she collapsed in
the house. From that moment on she did not leave the sick-
room at the top of the stairs. The children were quiet and
subdued, perhaps instinctively aware of what was happening
about them. Mrs Brontë rarely asked to see her children.
Attended by Patrick, she lived in great physical pain, and
the last seven months of her life were a nightmare. When
all six children fell ill with scarlet fever, Patrick himself came
close to the breaking point. The children recovered, but
Maria did not. She died in September 1821.

In November, Patrick wrote a letter to his old friend, the Reverend John Buckworth in Dewsbury. It is a tragic letter in every respect, not only for its description of the way his wife died, but for the implicit description of what that death had done to Patrick Brontë.

November 27th, 1821

My dear Sir,

I have just received yours of the 23rd., inst., and it is like good news from a far country or the meeting of old friends after a long separation. Your kind letter breathes that good sense, that Christian spirit and brotherly tenderness, which I have ever considered as prominent features in your character, and which are well-suited to soothe and benefit a mind like mine, which at present stands much in need of comfort and instruction. As I well know that you, as well as a much esteemed friend who is near to you, will take an affectionate interest in my affairs, whether they be prosperous or adverse, I will proceed to give you a brief narrative of facts as they have succeeded one another in my little sphere for the past twelve months.

When I first came to this place, though the angry winds which had previously been excited were hushed, the troubled sea was still agitated, and the vessel required a cautious and steady hand at the helm. I have generally succeeded pretty well in seasons of difficulty; but all the prudence and skill I could exercise would have availed me nothing had it not been for help from above. I looked to the Lord and He controlled the storm and levelled the waves and brought my vessel safe into the harbour. But no sooner was I there than another storm arose, more terrible than the former – one that shook every part of the mortal frame and often threatened it with dissolution. My dear wife was taken dangerously ill on the 29th of January last, and in a little more than seven months afterwards she died. During every week and almost every day of this long tedious interval I expected her final removal. For the first three months I was left nearly quite alone, unless you suppose my six little children and the nurse and servants to have been company. Had I been at Dewsbury I should not have wanted kind friends; had I been at Hartshead I should have seen them and others occasionally; or had I been at Thornton a family there who were ever truly kind would have soothed my sorrows; but I was at Haworth, a stranger in a strange land. It was under these circumstances, after every earthly prop was removed, that I was called on to bear the weight of the greatest load of sorrows that ever pressed upon me. One day, I remember it well; it was a gloomy day, a day of clouds and darkness, three of my little children were taken ill of a scarlet fever; and, the day after, the remaining three were in the same condition. Just at that time death seemed to have laid its hand on my dear wife in a manner which threatened her speedy dissolution. She was cold and silent and seemed hardly to notice what was passing around her. This awful season, however, was not of long duration. My little children had a favourable turn, and at length got well; and the force of my wife's disease somewhat abated. A few weeks afterwards her sister, Miss Branwell, arrived, and afforded great comfort to my mind, which has been the case ever since, by sharing my labours and sorrows, and behaving as an affectionate mother to my children. At the earliest opportunity I called in a different medical gentleman to visit the beloved sufferer, but all their skill was in vain. Death pursued her unrelentingly. Her constitution was enfeebled, and her frame wasted daily; and after above seven months of more agonising pain than I ever saw anyone endure she fell asleep in Jesus, and her soul took its flight to the mansions of glory. During many years she had walked with God, but the great enemy, envying her life of holiness, often disturbed her mind in the last conflict. Still, in general she had peace and joy in believing, and died, if not triumphantly, at least calmly and with a holy yet humble confidence that Christ was her Saviour and heaven her eternal home.

The children's aunt, Elizabeth Branwell, stayed in the home to care for them as best she could. But their mother was gone, and their father never recovered from his sorrow. The stoical and enterprising spirit that had brought Patrick from his humble home in Ireland was broken. At Haworth he gave up his cherished dream of literary success, and it did not occur to him that among his daughters there were those who would take the baton from his exhausted hands.

His only hope was that Branwell would carry on where he left off – but this was not to be.

Almost exactly a half of Patrick Brontë's life was spent at Haworth. He was forty-three when he arrived there and eighty-four when he died. The death of his wife, coming so soon after the family moved into the parsonage at Haworth, left Patrick a broken man. Up to that point he had cherished two dreams: one was to achieve literary success and fame; the other was to have a wife and family. The death of Maria blighted both of those ambitions. The books which bore his name as author were unknown outside his own small circle, and after leaving Thornton, Patrick wrote nothing more from his imagination. When Maria died, leaving Patrick with six small children, he clung for a few years to the idea of finding another wife who would be able to give him and his children the solid basis of a family life. His mind went back to those days at Wethersfield when he and Mary Burder had loved each other. In desperation he tried to remake the lost contact, but Mary Burder turned him down flat. Her letter was such a shock to Patrick that he could not bring himself to reply to it for five months.

When I look at your letter and see it in many parts breathe such a spirit of disdain, hatred and revenge, after the lapse of so long an interval of time, I appear to myself to be in an unpleasant dream; I can scarcely think it is a reality.

But it was a reality. With six young children he was not going to find a second wife. He gave up trying, and so began the second half of his life which is so different in spirit from the first half.

It is not within the scope of this book to describe the second half of Patrick Brontë's life. Many books have been written on the life of the family at Haworth, and there is little to add to what has already been written. Also, this book is not intended as a biography of Patrick Brontë, but as the story of his family and background. From this point of view, the second part of Patrick's life is the least interesting, and if his daughter Charlotte had not inherited her father's enormous enthusiasm it is extremely doubtful if the world would ever have heard of the Brontës. It is necessary here only to record the briefest details of Patrick's life at Haworth. If this book stimulates an interest in the lives of his children and the books they wrote, the choice of books available is vast.

In 1822 Patrick's mother died in Ireland. She was buried in the grounds of Drumballyroney Church, where her husband, Hugh, is buried. In 1825 a double tragedy befell Patrick. His eldest daughter, Maria, died on 6 May; and on 15 June his second daughter, Elizabeth, died. These deaths left Charlotte as the oldest surviving child, at the age of nine.

In 1842, Aunt Elizabeth Branwell, who had stayed with the family after the death of Patrick's wife, died at Haworth. Charlotte and Emily Brontë came home from Brussels too late to attend the sad funeral. Aunt Elizabeth left her small estate to her nieces, but her nephew Branwell was excluded. Patrick had failed miserably to instil into his son even a thousandth part of the discipline upon which his own life had been built. Branwell's life of drink and dissipation was ending in despair, for himself, and for all his family. He died on 24 September 1848. Three months later Emily died, and in the following year Anne died, leaving Charlotte alone with her father. Both of them were stunned with grief and haunted by their memories, but Charlotte was becoming a literary celebrity. Long after she had given up all hope of ever marrying, her father's curate, the Reverend Arthur Nicholls, proposed to her. The proposition was scorned by Patrick, who objected strongly to the idea of an impecunious Irish curate marrying his daughter. He had forgotten the time when he, also an impecunious Irish curate, had proposed to Mary Burder. However, Charlotte did marry her curate, on 29 June 1854. On 31 March 1855, Charlotte, who was pregnant and in her thirty-ninth year, also died, so Patrick was never a grandfather. Shortly before he died, at the age of eighty-four, he wrote the following words in a letter to an old friend.

Had I been numbered amongst the calm, sedate, concentric men of the world, I should not have been as I now am, and I should in all probability never have had such children as mine have been.

Patrick left his estate to Charlotte's widower; he also left forty pounds to be equally divided amongst his eight surviving brothers and sisters. The eldest sister of the family, Jane, had died in 1819. But the rest were alive and well, and living in Ballynaskeagh. The descendants of some of them live there today.

Chapter 10

Epilogue

When Patrick Brontë died at Haworth, the name Brontë, the
way he spelled the name, might well have died with him.
None of his children had issue, and the Brontës of Haworth
were the only branch of the family who spelled their name
in the way we know it today. In Ireland, Patrick's brothers
and sisters and their families spelled their name as Brunty
or Brontie. Even as late as 1897 there was a churchwarden
at Drumballyroney who wrote his name William Brontie;
and this was thirty-six years after the death of Patrick. But
as the fame of the Brontë sisters increased, so did the new
style of spelling the name. Gradually, between the end of
the nineteenth century and the First World War, all the
family began to spell their name as Brontë, and that is how
it has remained. It was natural enough, for after all, the
family knew they were related to the Haworth Brontës, and
as we have already made clear, the style of spelling did not
change the way the name was pronounced. The William
Brontie who was churchwarden at Drumballyroney in 1897
was the great-grandson of Patrick's brother William Brunty.
Yet the children of William, the churchwarden, wrote
their surname as Brontë, and they do so today. I have met
one of them; corresponded with others who are living in New
Zealand and Canada; and have had the pleasure of meeting
some of their children. Today the whole family are Brontës.

When researching the family history I learned that branches of the family went off to America, Canada, and New Zealand. The first emigration came, inevitably, at the time of the potato famine in 1845. This enormous disaster decimated the population of Ireland, where at least a million people starved to death; almost another million emigrated. This was out of a population of between eight and nine million! In terms of human misery it is shameful for those who ruled the country at the time, for the disaster could have been avoided. Nevertheless, it did happen, and there is scarcely a family in Ireland whom it did not touch.

A grandson of Patrick's brother William, named Joseph, emigrated to America. In all probability he was called Joseph Brunty. Another grandson of Patrick's brother William, by the name of Murphy Brunty, had a family of five children, who all emigrated to America. They were named William, James, Joseph, John, and Mary Anne. One of William's own sons, Matthew, emigrated to America and although a nephew of the Reverend Patrick Brontë, he would have been known as Matthew Brunty in America.

The list is by no means complete. The details of the family tree are sparse, but without any doubt at all there are descendants of the Brontës living in America today. I have seen a letter from an Eveline Brontë, dated 20 November 1892, from an address shown as Redwood, Deep River, Connecticut, addressed to 'Sweet dear darling Grandma', who was Mary Brontie (*née* Honna), the mother of the churchwarden at Drumballyroney in 1897. I cannot say how Eveline wrote her own surname because she merely signed the letter 'Eveline', but there will be many more Brontës or Bronties or Bruntys in America and perhaps a deeper research will be done after this book is published.

As regards the branch of the family in New Zealand there is already much more information available. One son of William, the churchwarden at Drumballyroney in 1897, is called Welsh Brontë. He emigrated to New Zealand and was

married there in 1939. His sister in Ireland very kindly gave
me her invitation card to the wedding, which was celebrated
on 7 June 1939, in St John's Church, Dannevirke. Welsh
Brontë was married to Alma Hannah. Now there is a son,
Roger Brontë, and two daughters, Carolyn and Shirley.
Roger Brontë travelled from New Zealand to Ballynaskeagh
a few years ago, and met his relatives there, before returning
to New Zealand, where he married and settled down.

In Ireland there are many descendants of the Reverend
Patrick's brother William. They form two branches which
are easily traced back to the marriage between William and
Jane Shaw. There were six sons and one daughter. One
branch stems from the marriage of one of the sons, Patrick,
to Catherine Murphy. The other stems from the marriage of
another son, William, to Mary Honna. The present generations of these branches of the family live in the area of Ballynaskeagh, only a short walk from the remains of the cabin
where the Reverend Patrick and his brother William were
born.

In July 1956 a ceremony was held on the site of the
remains of the cabin. Dr Phyllis Bentley, the novelist, un-
veiled a plaque which had been set inside the ruins. It was
the culmination of a great amount of work undertaken by
the Irish section of the Brontë Society, in association with
Banbridge District Council. At the ceremony were two
young girls, Emily and Anne Brontë. Both are now married,
with children of their own. When I visited the site in 1979,
my wife and I paced out the measurements of that 'neat Irish
cabin' about which Patrick Brontë wrote a poem. It
measured eighteen feet by twelve feet, with walls two feet
thick. It could be seen that there had been one dividing wall
creating the two small rooms, in one of which Patrick was
born. I was told that when the hearth-stone was dug out,
seeds of roasted corn had been found underneath.

I think that the road to Haworth begins at Magherally
Church, a couple of miles outside Banbridge. Today the

church is in ruins, but some of the gravestones were there on that summer day in 1776 when Hugh Brunty married his beloved Catholic girl Alice McClory. The walls of the church are standing, and it is possible to discern where the altar would have been when Hugh and Alice stood before it and made their vows.

The next point on the road is the place where they first set up home, the cabin at Imdel, near Ballynaskeagh. Close by is the ring of trees on top of the hill which is known as Imdel Fort. It was one of young Patrick's favourite places. The chapel and schoolhouse at Glascar Hill where Patrick first became a teacher are both in a fine state of preservation.

At Drumballyroney is the church where Patrick once preached to a crowded congregation of friends and family. The little schoolroom where Patrick had such success can have changed very little in the passing years. At the side of the schoolroom a grassy mound covers the graves of Patrick's father and mother, and many of his Irish family. A Brontë was recently interred there.

Finally, in Yorkshire, England, there is the parsonage and the church where Patrick's children lived out their lives. The village of Haworth will forever be associated with the name of Brontë.

It was in Haworth, and probably in the parsonage itself, that one of Patrick's daughters wrote the lines with which I end this book. But although I am sure that Emily Jane Brontë was in the parsonage when she wrote the lines, I feel equally sure that when she *thought* them, she was out on the wild moors where her soul lives, infinitely.

I lingered round them, under that benign sky: watched the moths fluttering among the heath and hare-bells; listened to the soft wind breathing through the grass; and wondered how anyone could ever imagine unquiet slumbers for the sleepers in that quiet earth.

A Brontë family tree

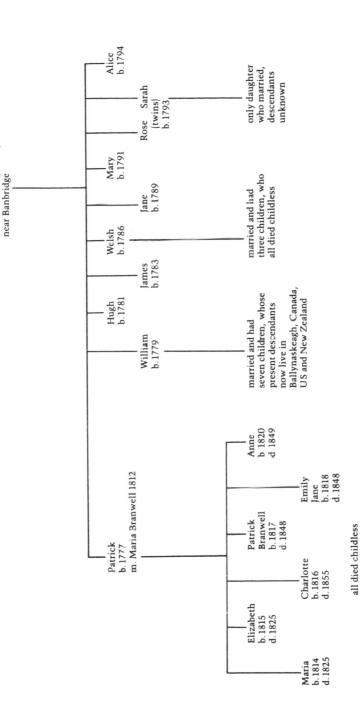

Hugh Brunty = Alice McClory
m. 1776 at Magherally Church
near Banbridge

Patrick
b. 1777
m. Maria Branwell 1812

William
b. 1779

Hugh
b. 1781

James
b. 1783

Welsh
b. 1786

Jane
b. 1789

Mary
b. 1791

Rose   Sarah
(twins)
b. 1793

Alice
b. 1794

married and had
seven children, whose
present descendants
now live in
Ballynaskeagh, Canada,
US and New Zealand

married and had
three children, who
all died childless

only daughter
who married,
descendants
unknown

Maria
b. 1814
d. 1825

Elizabeth
b. 1815
d. 1825

Charlotte
b. 1816
d. 1855

Patrick
Branwell
b. 1817
d. 1848

Emily
Jane
b. 1818
d. 1848

Anne
b 1820
d 1849

all died childless